# BUY MY BOOK

NOT BECAUSE YOU SHOULD,
BUT BECAUSE I'D LIKE
SOME MONEY.

# A
# WORTHLESS
## SELF-NO-HELP BOOK
### BY THE NO-AWARD-WINNING
*First Time Author John E Marszalkowski*

# BUY MY BOOK

NOT BECAUSE YOU SHOULD, BUT BECAUSE I'D LIKE SOME MONEY.

| | |
|---|---|
| Written by | John Edward Marszalkowski |
| | |
| Foreword by | Linda Giacchino |
| Guest Chapter by | Steve Keiller |
| Afterword by | Desiree Marszalkowski |
| About the Author by | Matthew Kopf |
| | |
| Editor | Angie West |
| Proofreader | Sara Merwin-Moe |
| Book Designer | Tegan Hendricks |
| Cover Designer | Jason Gierl |
| Cover Photographer | Jennifer Brindley |
| Chapter Photographer | Jennifer Janviere |
| Chapter Sculptor | James Richard Littleton |
| Illustrators | Christy Hall Watson |
| | Supple Jim Tierney |
| | Taylor Quinn |
| | Erin Maurice |
| | Annie Kassens |
| | Sarah Hetrick |
| | Ethan Chandler |
| | Will Sutton |
| | Kenneth Uzquiano |
| | Anja Notanja Sieger |
| | Matthew Kopf |
| | Elizabeth Gramz |
| | |
| Distributed by | Lulu Press, Inc |
| Published by | Barf-Bag Publishing |

BARF-BAG PUBLISHING

2018

First Printing: 2018

ISBN 978-1-7320226-1-4

BARF-BAG PUBLISHING
C/O ORPHONIC LLC
PO BOX 210454
MILWAUKEE WI 53221-8008

http://ThisIsAReal.Company

Ordering Information:

Special discounts are available on quantity purchases by corporations, associations, educators, and others. For details, contact the publisher at the above-listed address.

U.S. trade bookstores and wholesalers: Please contact Barf-Bag Publishing at the above-listed URL address.

# FOR CHARLOTTE

Have fun when you make money.
These suckers will buy anything.

Love,
Dad

```
       !]
       !
     #*(+$
       (
    -(++%$
       !
     +>{
      >^
    !<{]
     (<
     =_
   /![%<{]
    _![$
```

# TABLE OF CONTENTS

# ACKNOWLEDGEMENTS

The following are the people who passionately supported this project, so much so that they donated far more than the cost of their rewards to ensure this book was written.

### BIG DEAL SPONSORS

Kenneth Uzquiano

### CHAPTER SPONSORS

Jeffrey Niedzialkowski

Michael Uzquiano

Ryan Irons

### OTHER SPONSORS

Shane Olivo

Joshua Janis

# BUY MY BOOK
### NOT BECAUSE YOU SHOULD, BUT BECAUSE I'D LIKE SOME MONEY.

I'd like to acknowledge the first group of people who backed this book on the Kickstarter campaign. I won't say, "I couldn't have done this without you." However, I will say "I couldn't have paid for this without you."

- Jeremy Port
- Julie Kavanagh
- Vince "Moist Vomit" Verrinoldi
- Michael Heal
- Colleen Banach
- Madeline "Spirit Animal" Parker
- Andrew Kerber
- Angie West
- Elizabeth Gramz
- Christopher Stenner
- Luke Summerfield
- Greg Reynolds
- Lauren Brost
- Joshua Morrison
- Tracy Apps
- Samuel Morrison
- Dawn Borchardt
- Joseph Mlodik
- Rebecca Buchman
- Michael Bean
- Christy Watson
- Caitlin O'Gara
- Casey Abbot Payne
- Troy Freund
- Doug McGoldrick
- Stephanie Young
- Crystal Plahuta
- Nick Mitchell
- Michelle Sagert
- James Valona
- David Naida
- Erica Kowalski Weber
- James Richard Littleton
- Chelsea Goodnight
- Emma Rudd
- Brad De Pons
- Steve Keiller
- Jenn Romaniszak
- Katie White
- Supervisor Anonymous
- John Tyson
- Jessica Greenfield
- Scott Palkowski
- Professor Jon Friedland
- Brad "Black Belt" Bentley
- Matt Miller
- Hannah Hazelberg
- Bryan Conti
- Jen Huber
- Alexander Crowe
- Suzy Disi
- Hannah Karch
- Michael Dunn
- Abraham & Valarie Garcia
- "Anno Piano" Van Deusen
- Craig Sikora

# THANK YOU

I'd like to thank my family and friends for humoring me through this entire project.

Thanks to my wife Desiree for laughing at my jokes, even when they aren't great.

Thanks to those select friends who convinced me that my voice needs to be heard, reassured me more than once that I make quality content, and for believing in my unorthodox writing style. You know who you are. I also don't need to list your names because I already listed them in the acknowledgment section.

# FOREWORD

BY LINDA GIACCHINO

The day I met John Marszalkowski, I was a harried working mother just wanting to get off my feet. I came home to find this gangly kid named John in my house, hanging out with my youngest son, Ken. They made quite a pair, awkward shaggy-haired boys in their early teens, passionate about music, the future of animation, video games, and their ideas—of which they both had many. After you have read this book, imagine if you can, a house in which these kinds of conversations tumbled in ever-expanding rapids of sometimes loosely-related topics.

It was invigorating. A little crazy at times, but that's what teenagers do. They release energy into everything around them. That was John.

John lived in a different neighborhood, so Ken didn't meet him until he transferred from another school to the local middle school. Ken's father and I were in the middle of a contentious divorce, and Ken wasn't thriving at the private school we'd chosen for him. He was, and still is, artistic and free-spirited. If he didn't like a situation, he sulked and didn't apply himself. I feared for him, to be honest, and desperately wanted him to be happy in school. I'm a lifelong learner and introvert who doesn't often reveal her thoughts to others. Ken craved experiences and expressing himself. Maybe not to everyone, but he did it a lot. When it came to raising him, I made it up as I went.

I don't think Ken was more than two days at that middle school before he brought John home.

By the end of the week, John had become Ken's closest and best friend. It didn't take long to understand why. They bounced off each other like ping pong balls and, between them, covered a whole lot of ground. Their teachers. Movies. Best foods. Which creature was more useful: chickens or Chocobos? Lists of everything wrong with the world. Before long, they'd started a band in my basement, and the house was filled with their music and their friends. Male friends. Female friends. I went downstairs often enough to make sure they were only playing with music and not each other—but mostly I just left them alone.

As a writer, I understood how creativity thrives on benign neglect. That, and time. Children play. Young people create. John was a creator. It took only a few conversations with Ken about their music to see that John was the driving force of that band. He wrote most of the music. Ken became a drummer, but if he wrote any of the songs, he never told his mother about them. John's songs were good, and I still own the CDs he and his different bands made. I'm still not sure why they didn't make it big. I don't understand the music business.

Throughout Ken's high school years, John was something of a permanent fixture in our lives. My grocery cart soon included extra portions just in case John would be staying for dinner or a weekend. Don't even get me started on snacks. I'm pretty sure John and Ken were responsible for double-digit profit increases shown by the makers of Hot Pockets, Doritos, Tony's Pizza, and Pepsi products. Had I invested in Pepsi, I would have been a mogul before they ever graduated high school.

There were times I suspected he lived in the basement. Sometimes I'd just be sitting at the table, looking at the mail or whatever, and John would pop up, say, "Hi Mom!" and grab a bag of Doritos before disappearing back downstairs. I hadn't even known he was there. Whenever John's mother called to ask if he was there, my first instinct was always to say yes automatically. On almost every occasion, that was true. I got as used to calling John to the phone as I did my sons. He got used to calling me Mom because no one in that house ever called me anything else. John was, for all practical purposes, a member of the family.

After the boys graduated from high school, I saw less of John, but that was because life has a way of changing. A few years after my divorce, I met someone new and decided to make a change in my own life. Ken, following in his brothers' footsteps, went away to school. With no kids at home, I sold the house and moved to another state. John remained in Milwaukee to pursue his own life.

# BUY MY BOOK

## SO, WHY SHOULD YOU READ THIS BOOK?

Because John has written about that rarest of things people write about: an average guy's journey as an adult. He tells his own story without pulling a single punch. He also reveals an amazing inner life that takes day-to-day ordinariness and spins it into profound insights. A job is both opportunity and a kick in the nuts. John looks with clear eyes at some of our institutions and calls them out. Even the industry that is snack foods. He also examines loyalty, love, and what it means to be honest with oneself.

He's an artist with words as much as he ever was with music.

# INTRODUCTION

ILLUSTRATION BY CHRISTY HALL WATSON

# INTRODUCTION

This book has evolved quite a bit while I was writing it. It all started with just a name. The title "Buy My Book: Not Because You Should, But Because I'd Like Some Money" was written long before any intentions of mine were set into motion as to what the subject matter would be. All I knew was that I wanted to make a book, I wanted you to buy it, and I wanted to be very transparent about the fact that I needed to write it far more than you needed to read it. More than anything, I needed it to exist.

After the title was proclaimed publicly on my podcast show, the tone of the book was set in stone; humorous and not taking itself seriously.

The problem was that what I wanted to talk about was important. Luckily, my delivery is rarely serious.

The only point I initially wanted to make was that I wanted to write a book. I'd never done it before, and you have to try things sometimes—even when you know the results won't be excellent. The lesson of the book was the book itself (I think the kids call that META these days?).

After I finished the introduction that you are currently reading (yeah, I came back and added this part), I started a new topic of ranting about an industry I don't fully understand. Halfway through the chapter, I switched from trying to entertain you, to sitting on your couch and telling you about my childhood. I realized this was therapy.

I have been in and out of therapy my whole life, and the standard theme I get from it is that I'll talk a lot, they'll listen, they'll ask questions about what I said, and I'll discuss it some more. They never tell me what to do or what to think, but they get me to translate my thoughts into words, which helps me understand my feelings. Well, SHIT! I was paying them for that! In the form of a book, you're paying me! Writing this book is way better!

As I began to dump out my psychological baggage onto the page, I put something together; that all these thoughts, written in my voice, could serve an extremely important purpose. Even if I'm not an expert at what I'm talking about, my ramblings could potentially be priceless to a reader. And so, the book began to have a thesis. What is that thesis? Well, it's supposed to be a surprise, but if you want to get to the point of it all, skip ahead to chapter twenty-two.

Okay, so here was that original introduction:

It would seem that this book is here to serve almost no other purpose besides crossing "write a book" off my checklist. I mean, I'm glad you're here to witness this train-wreck. I don't think I've ever scored higher than a D+ in any English class I've ever taken, so I guess you're in for one wild ride of literary malarkey. I feel like I have a lot to say about many things, but each one wouldn't necessitate an entire book. So, you can look forward to a book that is pretty much all over the place.

In all seriousness, I have a voice, and I'm using it. I think you should use yours, too. I think many of us grew up in a world where almost everyone (including people who care about us) have made us feel like there are things we shouldn't do, things we shouldn't try, and things at which we will most certainly fail.

What I'd love to get across to you in this book is that none of those reasons are good enough. It's okay to fail. It's okay if the first thing you try kind of sucks. It's okay that you're not automatically good at anything. I'm a firm believer in the following statement, so I'm going to make the font bold…

## YOU HAVE TO MAKE SHITTY SHIT BEFORE YOU CAN MAKE GOOD SHIT.

And that's what we've done, together. You have participated in my experiment. You bought this piece-of-shit book. This book is my first book. It's not that good. It's probably not the worst book ever written, and you might find some value in it, but it's not perfect.

And that's fine. It had to start somewhere. You have to have a "first." Your "first" anything is allowed to suck.

The reviews of this book (if I can find anyone willing to review it) will probably be hilariously mean. You may feel stupider for having read it to completion. But that doesn't mean this book shouldn't exist. If ABSOLUTELY NO ONE finds ANY value in this book, I have still seen worth in writing it. So, honestly, I'm good.

So now, maybe the essential step in all of this: Money.

I want your money. You probably bought this book, so I have won that battle. I win the war when I sell enough copies to cover my costs and get at least one cent in the black. Do you know why that is important to me? It's not greed. It's simple; even though it will make people cringe, I will be able to call myself a professional author, technically. Eyes might roll, insults hurled, and even anger felt. I don't think those reasons are good enough to stop me from doing something I've always wanted to do.

If you don't think I should have written this book because you'd rather not see me make something that...

    a. doesn't hold up to your standards of what deserves to exist,
    b. could receive more praise than you think it should, or
    c. all of the above

... then the best advice I think I could give you would be to go fuck yourself, I suppose.

Now, I know that got pretty aggressive for a moment.

I'm sorry about that. That's not a message for you; it's for the haters. You're not a hater.

I think I like you a lot. I'm a sucker for flattery, so the fact that you are still reading this is a clear sign that you and I are going to get along great.

Without further ado, please, get a stiff drink, take off your pants, and please try to enjoy one of the worst books ever written.

```
]>#(%{_
   (]
    !
/>}+![({_
#><{%]{
```

# CHAPTER I

MARKETING IS STUPID, RIGHT?
OH WAIT, NO, IT'S ME.

ILLUSTRATION BY "SUPPLE JIM" TIERNEY

I think it's just the buzzwords that bug me. Maybe it's all the stupid job titles I see on LinkedIn. If your job title has any of these words in it, you can go directly to hell:

- Ninja
- Guru
- Evangelist (unless you work for a church)
- Innovator
- Champion
- Synergist

Either way, as I tried to think of ways to justify to you why you should be reading anything I write, I thought of describing myself as a "content creator." I immediately rolled my eyes.

A content creator was what I was when I was fifteen and didn't have a job. I wrote terrible music, I shot dumb videos, I designed simple websites, I drew awful comics and all sorts of content creation that didn't make me any money. In fact, a lot of that cost me money. So, forgive me, but it makes me think of something kids do for free. It's not how I ever pictured adults earning a living.

But apparently, it's a real thing, and I'd like to get me some of that money... Starting by writing this book, filled with the ridiculous ramblings of a man who failed all his high school English classes.

My buddy Steve and I recently started a podcast called "Who Are We To Podcast?" So far, we have no clear direction or agenda, but after receiving a small payment from our first sponsor, it occurred to me that I could make some amount of profit just for being myself and making things I want to make. Steve and I have been filming wedding videos and small business videos together since 2011, so we're familiar with professional content creation. However, it only recently occurred to me that, as opposed to creating something for a client, it's possible to make things for myself and still have clients, the idea being that your clients will find you.

Well, maybe. I don't know. I'll have to revisit this book after a while to see if I ever paid any of my bills with happiness.

Before I go back to talking trash about people who work in marketing, let me say that I kind of like some marketing stuff.

For years I was in local rock bands. I never realized it at the time, but making music was not exactly my favorite part of making music... if that makes any sense.

I like making things, and I love showing it to people, hoping to hear someone say, "that doesn't suck. I want more!" which, of course, gives me motivation and purpose to make more. It doesn't matter what it is. Here is what I loved about being in shitty bands:

**Not Marketing. At least I don't think it is.**

- Meeting up with good friends for very unproductive band practices
- Writing and recording original songs
- Networking with venues and other musicians
- Getting the free beer at shows

**Marketing, right? Maybe some of this is. I don't know.**

- Creating/maintaining a website and social media sites for the band
- Setting up e-commerce for album sales
- Contacting record labels and radio stations by finding cost-effective ways to design mailers that creatively grabbed their attention
- Organizing photoshoots and videos

Working with artists to develop logos, web graphics, album layouts, and other merchandise.

Trying to come up with creative ways to move a thousand copies of an album for which there was virtually no demand.

So, yeah, all-in-all there is a lot more work that goes into making lousy music than some people would guess. It never really felt like work, though. It was the part I wanted to do.

Forcing myself to sit down and write songs was the hardest part if I had to call any part of it "work." Knowing that new songs were what people expected— that made it feel like work, for some reason.

Okay, back to talking shit about people in marketing.

It seems to me that there could be a lot of things in the marketing field that I might find enjoyable. What I don't understand is what it is they do. You can't just ask them. You'll get a spiel that doesn't answer the question, to which I want to respond with, "what observable accomplishments did you achieve today between the hours of 9 am and 5 pm?"

Or, to quote Bob from the movie Office Space,

*"What would ya say... ya DO here?"*

Don't get me wrong; I admire that. I've never really been good at getting x-amount of work done in y-amount of time. Besides what I already do, I can't name one single career that doesn't require accomplishing a specific amount of something before the end of time. If someone can collect a paycheck by basically just being helpful by letting a company better understand who their clients are and how to advertise to them, good for them, I guess.

Maybe I'm not mad at marketers as much as I'm a little jealous of them. I know I shouldn't be, though. I'm sure they hate their jobs just like most people do. I cringe when I stop to imagine myself working at some firm, and a folder gets thrown on my desk, and the boss says,

"Hey Marszalkowski, we need to figure out what kind of toilet paper is primarily being bought by people who shop the ethnic aisle at grocery stores.

Get me a report on ways to position product placement so that we can sell more Charmin to people who are buying taco sauce."

That probably isn't at all what marketing people do. I didn't research this at all.

I shouldn't flatter myself with even entertaining the idea that a career like that is an option for me. Not that I couldn't do it. I believe that I could learn it and do it. I don't think I could resist the urge to drop out of college again, in an attempt to obtain some bullshit degree that is required.

I've never done well in traditional classroom settings. I only recently figured out what learning style works best for me[1], and I wish I had figured it out years and years ago when I was failing pretty much every class that wasn't music or art.

I spent my entire youth believing that I was an idiot because I could never absorb information and regurgitate it the same way other kids did. I thought I had a learning disability and told myself that I'd never succeed in college (I tried and failed) so I'd never have a good job, and I'd always have a hard life[2].

---

[1] In case you were wondering about that learning style, this is what I very recently became aware of: I learn very well when I study something that I fully intend to reteach to someone else. It helps me immensely if it's something I want to know, but that isn't required. For whatever reason, I absorb information differently when I know that I'll be explaining it to someone, later on, to help that person understand it (please note that's different than being orally quizzed by someone who already knows the information). Knowing I'll have the opportunity to sound like I know what I'm talking about gets me excited enough to spend that extra effort understanding it. Or maybe I want to feel helpful? Or perhaps I'm a know-it-all that knows very little. Who knows? Only my psychologist knows for sure!

I mean it when I say "extra effort." I'll still need to reread chapters over and over. I'll continue to need to restart lessons. I'll even need to do extra research. I'll need to spend way more time on it than it should take because now I need to understand it for my reasons, not just because I should.

I think I convinced myself that I was too stupid to be happy. I wish I could go back in time and tell myself that I can do almost anything I want to do, but some things are just going to be harder. So, if I want to do it, I probably won't mind working harder for it anyways.

Wait. How did I get off topic so much? How did I go from hating on marketing to why I graduated from public school with a 1.0 GPA? Well, I guess I was trying to hit a bunch of birds with one stone for the first chapter. That is that I am not well-educated, my resume looks terrible, I'm a creative person, I like to work hard on particular things, and I have some of the worst Attention Deficit Disorder you'll ever read in book form. Now, since I've set the bar pretty low and made it abundantly clear that I'm not qualified to act like a know-it-all by any traditional concepts of informational authority, let's move on to chapter two.

---

[2] I'd like to give a quick shout-out to all my amazing teachers that had to put up with my bullshit. If you're reading this, please know that you're part of the reason I grew up to be a decent human being. I know you had to work with a lot of dented cans over the years, and I want you to know that I didn't turn out to be a complete shithead. Thank you for encouraging me to follow my interests. For never making me feel like the idiot that I thought I was. You're also part of the reason why I've never been to jail or become addicted to drugs. That said, I think the educational system failed me... but you didn't... if that makes any sense.

Also; fuck you, Mr. Thompson.

# WORKSHEET TIME!

Oh, SNAP! This book is interactive!

That's right; you can either dive into the experience by filling out this worksheet or by ignoring it. Either way, can you imagine how short this book would seem if I didn't stick fillers like this in it?

Okay, here we go...

- List the parts of your life at work, home, and other places where you are awesome at what you do.

- List the parts of your life in which you suck.

- If you could create a custom role for yourself in life, where your tasks are only things you excel at, and everything else is delegated to someone else, what would that look like for you?

# CHAPTER II

I'M NOT SUICIDAL, I JUST OFTEN THINK
ABOUT WHAT WOULD HAPPEN IF I CRASHED
MY CAR INTO A BRIDGE EMBANKMENT.

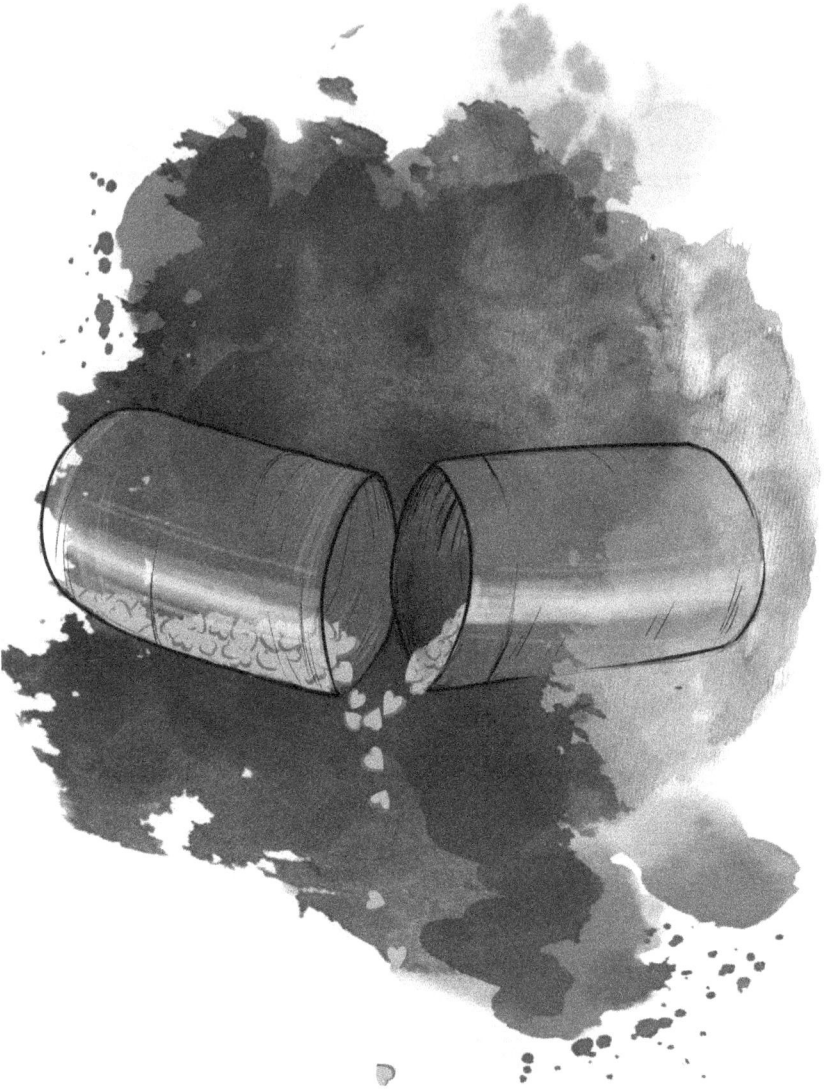

ILLUSTRATION BY TAYLOR QUINN

This chapter is brought to you in part by clinical depression, but also a synthetic feeling of happiness caused by a dose of Sertraline that just kicked in.

I've currently placed myself in an unfortunate spot on the Darwinian scale of things. I haven't been physically active. I've been making poor meal choices. I'm always making decisions that ultimately negatively affect me. The only reason I've survived this long is that (lucky for me) we live in a society that doesn't require survival of the fittest... at least, not in the traditional sense.

I've still managed to dupe a beautiful woman into marrying me, mating with me, and allowing my genes to be carried on in an adorable kid.

Need proof that society has deactivated survival of the fittest? Well, for starters, if I die, my family gets a pretty decent life-insurance check. Dying can be more helpful to my offspring than being a provider.

I joke, but it's going to be a lot of hard work to save up enough money to pay for her Harvard* education. My wife and I are going to have to do a lot of hunting and gathering for the rest of her youth.

Or... I could die. I kid, but it seriously puts things into an interesting perspective if you've always believed that hard work pays off. I can (literally) lay on the couch and eat myself to death, and that will generate more income for my family than I ever could earn.

Okay, let me fix that awkward feeling you might be having right now if you are a person that cares about me. I love my life. I love being alive. I want to stay alive for a very long time. The world (as I know it) is a beautiful place. The

---

*She does not need to go to Harvard. That's not an expectation I'm trying to set. I simply wanted to pick a fancy college for this example to exaggerate the higher potential costs of education. At the time of me writing this, Harvard is a fancy-schmancy college. A quick Google search tells me that a four-year education there costs just over $250,000... the exact amount of money my fat-ass is insured for up until the end of her fourth year. That's an amount that is 100% more than I'm personally able to earn for her.

fact that I was that one-in-a-trillion sperm that made it to the egg is fantastic. What a tremendous opportunity this is to be alive at all... but to be born into a first-world country? That's something so miraculous that I don't even know how to appreciate it appropriately. But above any of that, I love the people in my life so much, and I'd do anything for them... and that certainly includes staying alive.

I suffer from depression, but not continuously and usually not to such extreme extents that would include suicidal thoughts. I often wonder how a narcissist like myself can have such low self-esteem. I mean, I'm writing a book about myself, for Pete's sake! How self-obsessed do I have to be to think people would want to read me writing about myself?

And yet, even when I think the world revolves around me, I often feel that I am pure shit. I don't care for myself as a person. I wouldn't want to be friends with me. And when I try to change who I am to fit what I want to be, I'm often overwhelmed by the depressing reality that I'm not capable of negotiating the obstacles of becoming anything but pure shit.

Luckily, as I said before, I've figured out how my shitty existence can exist in society. And so, I'm not suicidal.

I'm happy to be alive, and in a beautiful world with beautiful people. I've learned how to avoid feeling like a failure by just preventing certain types of challenges, like being healthy or going to job interviews. If I had tried writing a good book, I could have failed. But I decided to write a terrible book... so I could only screw this up with it being well-received.

## CONFIDENCE

I just watched an interview with entrepreneur Gary Vaynerchuk, and it inspired me to add a section to this chapter about confidence. Gary has an abundance of it, and I think people could debate if he deserves as much as he has.

What bugs me about confidence: Too many people have it who don't deserve it, and too many people need it for mental health. For example, my wife noticed that my self-esteem had been on the decline when I shared with her a request I sent to a tattoo artist, asking for her help with art for this book. Here is what I sent her:

*"Not a tattoo request, but would you have any interest in doing an illustration for a chapter in my book I'm writing? It's a shitty book, and it doesn't deserve your talent. That said, I respect you, and you deserve better offers than bullshit like this, so please say no if this message made you roll your eyes at all. I'm so sorry for wasting your time."*

Now, I feel like this kind of fits right in with the tone of the book. In general, I've learned that it's always best to set the bar as low as possible in life and then outperform anyone's expectations. I commonly hear it said as "Under-promise, over-deliver." Perhaps I take it a step too far, or maybe my real doubt of self-worth shines through in my comedy, but one thing is sure—I do not deserve more confidence.

Let me explain that with more details because it might sound more negative than I meant it.

Let's imagine that a university philosophy professor started sharing with you their opinions on the meaning of life, but they kept saying things like "But who am I to speak of such things?" Wouldn't that bug you a little? Wouldn't you want to say, "You, of all people, should get to speak about this topic with confidence, even though the answer to that pointless question is subjective."

Now imagine this time that some absolute nobody, with a sixth-grade education, who starts a vlog on YouTube about world politics, proceeds to lecture the masses on what would solve that whole Middle-East dilemma. You'd want to punch that idiot in the mouth, wouldn't you?

In these scenarios, you have one person who is qualified to speak on a subject and so clearly deserves more confidence. Then you have this other person who doesn't. I'm not saying the second person shouldn't speak their opinions confidently... but to say they deserve that confidence is a bit of a stretch if you ask me. They should have whatever healthy amount of confidence is appropriate for half-decent self-esteem. They aren't entitled to more, but they could be in need of more.

I'm not a psychologist. I have no idea what fixes self-esteem issues. Otherwise, I'd be practicing whatever that is. But if someone has a shallow opinion of their views, chances are it would be good for their self-esteem to raise their confidence. However, this is not the same thing as saying that this person deserves to be confident. They might not. They deserve to be well-balanced in their brain, but it doesn't change their qualifications.

At the cost of being long-winded, I'll conclude with this thought: Everyone is entitled to have confidence in voicing their opinions, so long as their views are not presented as "truth." Now and then, I'll find myself going into rant/lecture-mode, and I'll regret it, because while I'm happy that I voiced my opinions confidently, sometimes I'll do so in a matter-of-fact way that makes me cringe in retrospect.

I hate know-it-alls. Sometimes, when I permit myself to display confidence, I'll back down out of fear of sounding like a know-it-all. I don't know who initially said the following, but I've been repeating it so long that I might as well try to say it's my quote:

*"The things we find annoying in others are what we don't like about ourselves."*

So, I come to this weird contradictory crossroads where I need more confidence for better self-esteem, but every step toward that goal puts me one step closer to becoming something I can't stand. So, in a way, what I want to be is someone with low self-esteem. That can't be good.

But who am I to speak of such things?

# DEATH

Since I started writing this book, several friends have passed away. They were relatively young and too young to die. They were my age. I hadn't seen some of them for years, but we went way back.

One of those friends just died while this book was being edited, and I'm adding this sentence to a completed manuscript with tears in my eyes.

A handful of years ago a childhood friend passed away. He was the first friend I ever had and had been one of my best friends for the majority of his life.

That one messed me up pretty bad.

I wish it were something we could push off to the end of our priority list, but it doesn't work that way. I mean, that makes sense; you do everything you are going to do in your life, then the very last thing you do is die. So, naturally, the longer your list is of things you need to do, the longer you'll live. A life like that, on paper, seems perfect. It doesn't work that way at all. While we can make decisions that affect our probability of survival, there are apparent forces outside of our control that can cut things short for any of us.

And so, it's been becoming clear to me that we (adults of any age) can no longer hold the passive perspective that...

- We will die someday,[3] which is not today.
- It will happen a long time from now. Certainly, long after the age of eighty.[4] Probably right around one-hundred.[5]
- We'll die after we've done everything we wanted to do.[6]

---

[3] *You should include today and right now as a possibility.*

[4] *US life expectancy is, on average, less than 79 years of age.*

[5] *Only 0.0173% of Americans live to the age of 100.*

[6] *You'll likely give up on the rest of your goals when your health begins to fail*

- Our passing won't negatively affect anyone else psychologically,[7] financially,[8] or in any way outside of normal mourning.
- It will either be in our sleep[9] or if we are awake[10] it will resemble Yoda becoming one with the force.
- We certainly won't be in pain, afraid, or alone when it happens.
- There is a 0% chance we will be murdered.[11]
- All our children and grandchildren will survive us.

And the list keeps going.

And so, I've concluded that it's time to get my shit together, figuratively. If I die unexpectedly, I don't want it to be a burden on my family and friends. I want it to go as smoothly as possible. I want to get my shit together, so that even if I died today, people would say, "His life was cut short, but his life was top shelf, baby!"

To which someone would reply "I know, right? His life had a five-star review on Amazon, even without the extended warranty."

It takes some severe getting-together-of-shit to be able to plan your funeral the way I'd like to. I'm going to need to reserve an animal wrangler for the wake because I want to have a variety of baby animals there for people to pet

---

[7] *The bereaved that suffer grief, which disrupts their functioning for over a month, meet the criteria for a major depressive episode.*

[8] *The average American traditional funeral costs an average of $8,500. In addition to that, a life insurance policy (for the annual fiscal impact you have on your partner/dependents, multiplied by ten) is ideal.*

[9] *Only 1 in 8 people die in their sleep.*

[10] *I haven't found anything to indicate this ever even happens if dying of natural causes.*

[11] *In America, there is a 1 in 20,000 chance you will be murdered. This might not seem too bad, but imagine going to a sold-out sports stadium once a year, watching five people in attendance get executed each time, then thinking: "I like my odds. This is fine."*

and hold. You can't be sad if you're carrying a joey (baby koala). I'll also need to book a few stand-up comedians to roast me.

I'm also not sure of how the logistics of this will work, but I want my remaining (unharvested) body parts to be turned into a mushroom farm, or crammed into a giant potted plant with a Redwood sapling. Then, plant it in a national park with a sign that says, "Please, I need nutrients! Johnny ate way too much garbage! Please, piss on me!"

Before I can plan my epic funeral, I need to get a lot of things in order. I guess that all has to start right now since we never know when we have to "go on vacation" (as Momma Gump so terribly defined it).

# WORKSHEET TIME!

List ten things you like about yourself.[12] This does not mean ten things you think you're better than others at, but it can be things you think you are good at.

_____

_____

_____

_____

_____

_____

_____

_____

[12] *A therapist once asked me this. I could not answer, and this question still haunts me to this day.*

# CHAPTER III

I THINK EVERYONE IS WRONG ABOUT GODS
AND GOVERNMENT, BUT LET'S NOT KILL
EACH OTHER, PLEASE.

ILLUSTRATION BY CHRISTY HALL WATSON

# WARNING:

**THIS CHAPTER IS EVERYTHING I AM NOT SUPPOSED TO TALK ABOUT AT FAMILY EVENTS OR WORK.**

**IF YOU ARE CURIOUS ABOUT MY PERSPECTIVE, PLEASE READ THIS CHAPTER. HOWEVER, IT IS VERY POSSIBLE I DO NOT AGREE WITH YOU REGARDING SOMETHING ABOUT WHICH YOU FEEL DEEPLY PASSIONATE.**

**PLEASE KNOW THAT JUST BECAUSE WE MIGHT NOT AGREE ON SOMETHING, THAT DOESN'T MEAN I DON'T LOVE AND RESPECT YOU.**

Before I even start talking about religion and politics, I want to start off by talking about Burden of Proof and an analogy for it that I've been developing over the years. It's not perfected yet, but this book isn't going to wait for it to be polished. Fair warning: I'm about to beat a dead horse to a pulp.

## ARGUMENTUM AD IGNORANTIAM

A person who you have never met walks up to you on the street and proceeds to tell you that...

"I have 37 cents in my right pocket." To which you might respond with something like,

"Oh, okay, if you say so."

After all, this information doesn't seem essential, and this person doesn't seem untrustworthy. But, for some reason, this claim is more important than that. Let's say the stranger urgently responds with,

"No, you don't get it, there is exactly 37 cents in my right pocket. It's a fact. I believe it is true. If you don't also believe it is true, then you are wrong."

Now this gets you just a tiny bit defensive, right?

You might respond with a request for proof. Maybe now you feel skepticism where you didn't before, and proclaim that you do not share the stranger's belief that 37 cents is in their right pocket. I don't know how you think, but some of you might even go a full one-eighty and declare there is not 37 cents in their pocket unless proven otherwise. To all of this, the stranger replies,

"I need you to trust me. I can feel the 37 cents in my pocket. I know it's there. I've heard it rattling around in there ever since I put these pants on. I want to share it with you, but for me to do that, you must first believe that 37 cents is in my right pocket."

So again, you ask to see it, but they shake their leg and ask that you try and hear the rattle. The stranger asks you to touch their leg and feel its presence. To which you say,

"No!"

Obviously. This encounter is starting to get ridiculous. You're not going to start touching a stranger's leg and putting your ear up to their hips so that you can agree that their claim is valid. But let's say you humor them and you do. And you concede that,

"Yeah, I hear something. I feel something. But that doesn't mean it's 37 cents. It could be your keys. It could be 36 cents. It could be 37 pesos (which is not only different but not even close to being worth the same thing). I don't think you are trying to trick me. You seem sincere, and I believe that you believe there is 37 cents in your pocket. I am just without that belief. To have that belief, I would need to see proof."

This perspective is vital in the branding of atheism. I think atheism is too often perceived as opposition to faith when in reality it is an extremely vague title, and a lot of views fall under its umbrella. In my analogy, the stranger believes there is 37 cents in their pocket. They might be right, or they might be wrong, but regardless, they believe it. You then either think the stranger is correct, or you don't think they are correct. Not assuming that they are right is DIFFERENT than believing they are wrong. You might often hear that an atheist requires as much faith as a believer to think there is no god. That's partially true if you word it like that. However, being without a belief in something is not the same thing as believing it doesn't exist.

The only reason I use the 37 cents analogy is that gods'/God's existence is a very touchy subject for many people and many people have been brought up to treat atheism like a "bad" word. Using an analogy that disconnects the emotion from it is sometimes the only way I can get across my passionate view on atheism. That view is simply:

If you are not a theist, you are an atheist.

Or, here is a fun tongue twister to try and say three times fast:

A theist is not an Atheist... a *theist* is not an *atheist*... a theist is not an atheist.

That's the end of this category description. Being an atheist does not make you an anti-theist.[13] It doesn't make you a liberal.[14] It doesn't mean you subscribe to any "creed" besides that you are without the belief in god/gods.

---

[13] *Anti-theism is a subcategory of atheism, but not all atheists are anti-theists.*

[14] *I went to an atheist convention in Minnesota years ago (hosted by the American Atheist Association) because Richard Dawkins was speaking. I heard a variety of different views from the atheists in attendance. Some were pro-choice, and some were anti-choice. Some were fiscally conservative, and some were not. Views on foreign policy were all across the board. While it's obvious that the Republican Party's positions (aimed at religious voters) make most atheists "not Republican," it doesn't technically have anything to do with politics.*

It's important to word it this way because it emphasizes that the theist is making the CLAIM. A "theist" identifies as someone who believes in a god or gods. They have a belief, and they make a claim. Either you think there is a god, or you don't. There isn't any gray area here. If you aren't sure if there is a god, then you don't believe there is, in fact, a god, so your views are not theistic. You haven't ruled out the existence of a god, but you haven't wholly subscribed to the belief.

Imagine you knock on the door of a private theist club, and a security guard comes to the door and asks, "Do you believe in a god?" If you say anything besides "yes" to the security guard, then he doesn't let you in. If you say "maybe," he doesn't let you in. If you say "probably," he doesn't let you in. If you say "I'm 99% sure"... you guessed it: he doesn't let you inside. The only people that get inside and get to participate in theism are the people that answer that question with the single word, "yes."

EVERYONE ELSE IS OUTSIDE. If you're not in the theism building, you are outside of it. That is atheism: WITHOUT theism.

To "show my math" on this one, let me change up the scenario: You walk up to a club, and the security guard asks, "Do you believe there is no god?" Those that answer "yes" are let inside. Everyone else is outside. Guess who is out there? The theists are, yes, but so are many atheists. That's because this is a very exclusive club. It's not the club of atheism. It's a subset of atheism that has a much more specific dress code. And so, some atheists are still outside.

Still not getting it? One last comparison: A member of The Alliance of Baptists knocks on the door of the Westboro Baptist Church. The Westboro Baptist who answers the doors asks, "Does God hate fags?" to which the Alliance Baptist responds, "no" and is not let inside. They are both Christian Baptists, but you have to be a particular kind of asshole to get inside the Westboro Baptist Church. Fun fact about Baptists that I wasn't aware of until I wrote this: The Alliance of Baptists was formed in 1987 as the Southern Baptist Alliance by Liberal individuals and congregations who were considering separating from the Southern Baptist Convention as a result of the Conservative resurgence/fundamentalist takeover controversy. Liberal Baptists: I didn't know that was a thing. Well, isn't that something?

## RAISED RELIGIOUSLY

I had been raised Catholic, and I was totally into it for most of my childhood. It certainly made life enjoyable, believing that supernatural powers were intervening with everyone's natural reality. It was comforting to know that when life sucked terribly, at least someday you get to die and everything will be all better. In fact, it gave me the only positive feelings I've ever felt at a funeral when I was missing someone so much. When evil people got away with evil acts, it was satisfying to believe they couldn't escape justice in the afterlife. And above all of that, for a kid with low self-esteem, who always thought he was unlovable, it was alleviating to know God loved me.

Faith was a sweet drug at the time but looking back I'm pretty much convinced that it was a placebo. And knowing now that it was a placebo makes it impossible ever to feel the placebo effects again. Just how I can't make Christmas feel more magical by deciding to believe in Santa Claus.

As of recently, I've subscribed to a "coexist" attitude. Except for children and young adults, I'd say most of us are pretty set in our ways. Those are the people who move in next door to you, who you work with, and who you need to interact with within our society. That means that I don't want to purposely try to make people feel bad or speak condescendingly toward them. I want to treat them with respect. I want them to treat me with respect. I will think they are wrong about some things and they will think I am wrong about some things.

And that's fine. That's diversity. That's what America is all about (or should be). And yet, many of us take every opportunity to either attempt to convert others to our views, or we publicly voice our opinions like they are facts.[15]

The idea that we can convert the views of those around us to match ours sure sounds convenient and would probably be very satisfying, but it also kind of makes you that asshole that goes around answering questions that no one is asking you.

I think we should learn to coexist with everyone over the age of 25 or something. That doesn't mean we can't show other people our views and be open to seeing other people's perspectives.

---

[15] *Please note that I didn't say, "we voice our truths like they are facts," because facts are facts. Assuming there are individual-truths is screwing around with semantics. I hate the fact that we can use the same words and they mean different things to different people. Well, this is my book, and there is no room for argument, so let me set the record straight on this issue. Or rather, the semantics I prefer.*

*Facts are true for everyone, even if you don't agree or if you can't see them from your perspective. The natural world is operating on a long list of laws, and scientists have identified many of them.*

*Truths are often seen as a perspective, relative to their context, and immune to ignorance. Like the idea that two people could be looking at a number painted on the ground from opposite positions. One person sees a six, and the other person sees a nine. They are both "right" from their perspectives, but relative to numbers five and seven beside it, only the person stating it is a six is telling "the truth" based on supporting evidence.*

*However, the person stating it is a nine is also telling "the truth" if they are ignorant to its surrounding five and seven. They aren't lying; they believe it to be a nine because they are unaware of the context.*

*I think most of the time when people are stating "the facts," what they are saying is what they believe to be true. And there is nothing wrong with that, so long as they are not ignoring context and supporting evidence.*

*So, all that means is that saying "the truth is" should be equal to saying "the fact is" and should not be used to mean "to the best of my knowledge," although it often is used that way.*

It means that we aren't changing other people's minds. We only change our minds. Kids on the other hand, well, they don't know everything; they think they do. Debates are healthy. Arguments can be productive. For those who are continuously learning, they are perpetually learning about themselves and evolving their worldview. That's not everyone. Learn to pick your battles.

> *"If someone doesn't respect evidence, what evidence are you going to give them to prove that they should respect it? If someone doesn't value logical consistency, what logical argument are you going to give them that will demonstrate that they should?" – Sam Harris*

## POLITICS

In the first half of this chapter, I could confidently speak about what I lack in religious beliefs. I consider myself an expert on atheism because it's effortless to be an expert on your perspective regarding anything in which you are without belief. However, I'm not confident in speaking about politics, as it is immensely more complicated than just acknowledging that with which you don't agree.

That doesn't stop me from voicing what I think about politics, though. Like most Americans, despite my ignorance, I still manage to think I have the answers. This is normal, right?

I'd never want to debate any issues because outside of my opinions, I am not an authority on the government, the economy, foreign relations, or you name it. I can primarily only defend my point of view on social issues.

Okay, I just wanted to get that out of the way before I make an ass out of myself. If I've set the bar low enough, please proceed.

## THE PERFECT CANDIDATE

I've been trying to figure what it would take to build the perfect presidential candidate. What hard stances can the "other side" of the aisle live with/ without (for both sides)? Would enough people ever vote for a third party?

The country feels so split that we think we can so quickly lump people into a left or a right category. Third parties are more like subcategories of the two major parties and don't necessarily hold different positions.

Libertarians, for example, are (when oversimplified and generalized,) fiscally conservative and socially liberal, in that with both cases, they seem not to give a fuck about other people. When you consider that element of the Libertarian platform, it's a refreshing concept. It might be a relief to stop worrying about everyone else for a second and worry about yourself. Luckily for humanity, I think enough people's hearts bleed for their countrymen that they would reject living in an Anarchistic Mad Max society. Having so little government puts Libertarianism right of the Republican, even when you consider the strong Voluntaryism values that many Libertarians hold.

The Green party isn't a third party, either. I'm convinced that it exists to make the Democratic Party seem more centrist. Fun fact: I've taken the surveys at ISideWith.com a few times, and every time it says my views line up with the Green party by over 90%. That doesn't make the Green party a real option for me. It reminds me that I am the opposite of a Republican.

I think Bernie Sanders was refreshing, partly because he was different than your typical democrat. That's because he wasn't a typical Democrat; he is a Democratic Socialist. It gave us that third party vibe, but again it was still just a subcategory of the left, not an alternative to the two-party system. I think it was appropriate to run as a Democrat because running as a third party would not have honestly been an alternative option. Hillary (Clinton) was left. Bernie (Sanders) was more left. In a perfect world, Bernie should have won the Democratic nomination and moved on to destroy (Donald) Trump, but something fishy happened with the Democratic Party. I'm not sure what, but something seemed off about the primaries. I don't know. Do your research on that one. Anyways...

Here is the problem I think there would be with a third party option: they wouldn't represent the majority of Americans.

Currently, either a Democrat or a Republican will win and, usually, it's pretty close, like 51% to 49%. Even though it's almost split down the middle, the president USUALLY represents the majority of the voters (except for when the electoral vote is being dumb).

So, what would happen if there was a STRONG third party option? Let's say the third party candidate barely wins the vote? For example, 34%-33%-33%.

While something like this might be refreshing to see after all the problems with the two-party system, it would mean that the president now only represents about a third of the American voters.

So, for the first time, our president-elect would not have been voted for by the majority of the voters.

One of the significant problems with the two-party system is that I think we vote against someone more than we vote for someone. In the case of the last election, I believe this is what happened:

- 23% of Americans voted against Hillary by voting for Trump.
- 24% of Americans voted against Trump by voting for Hillary.
- 3% of Americans voted against the two-party system.
- 50% of Americans voted against everyone by not voting.

Hillary won the popular vote with 2.86 million more votes than Trump, but the electoral college slept in and failed to prevent a tyrant from taking office, officially proving the electoral college worthless.

So, when I look at how many people didn't vote, it's easy to see that the president (regardless of who would have won) doesn't represent the majority of Americans ANYWAYS.

I guess we might as well have strong third-party options, because the president may never have the support of most Americans ever again.

If we are potentially always electing someone who doesn't represent most of us, then we might as well start figuring out how we can select the perfect compromise: Someone that no one completely agrees with, but someone most people think is a fair representation of the interests of most Americans.

We need to start thinking about what issues are the most important ones for the nation, not just what problems affect us personally. What are we willing to bend on? What issues can we turn a blind eye to for the greater good, and what issues are there for which we should fight?

## GUNS

Well, it's that time again. There has been another school shooting. It's already a sad point that I can't just write that it's the school shooting. It's unfortunate that I can't even write the school shooting of 2018. No, at the time of typing this, this is the EIGHTH fatal school shooting of 2018. Heartbreakingly, there will most certainly be more.[16]

I don't consider myself to have a ground-breaking perspective on the gun/violence issues in America. I haven't researched this subject to any degree, besides just listening to a variety of opinions from a non-variety of people who are all in the same bubble as me. And that is something along the lines of, *"Guns are bad because they kill people, but if they didn't, they would be awesome."* I think that is a solid point based off one specific experience I have: NERF guns are fucking awesome.

I haven't fact-checked this, but I'm going to go out on a limb and assume that no one has ever been killed with a NERF gun. As a kid, few things were less fun than shooting foam balls and suction-cup-darts at your friends.

The more ammo that your NERF gun held, the better.

---

[16] *Since writing this part and finishing the rest of the book, there has been 15 more school shootings that resulted in injuries and/or fatalities. As of May 25th, 2018 there has been a total of 23 school shootings in America this year alone.*

The faster it shot, the better.

The more PSI of impact that it had on your target, the better.

For me, it's clear why adults like guns. It's pretty much for the same reason all kids like NERF guns.

Except now we are supposed to be older and more responsible, so we can upgrade our ammo from foam balls to lead bullets. We're old enough to go out into a rural area and blow up watermelons with hand-canons. We can blast bottles off a fence at long distances. If this is why (or part of why) you like guns, then cool. You should. You can add other reasons to it, but at its core foundation, guns are indisputably awesome. I don't want to rip off Jim Jefferies' bit on this entirely, but he's right. Here, I'll quote him:

*"There is one argument and one argument alone for having a gun, and this is the argument...*

*'Fuck off. I like guns.'*

*It's not the best argument, but it's all you've got. And there's nothing wrong with it. There's nothing wrong with saying,*

*'I like something. Don't take it away from me.'"*

The problem I have with grownup-NERF is that it requires a particular type of individual using guns for everything to make sense: a law-abiding citizen with little-to-no anger management issues, and perfect mental health. Someone who doesn't experience road-rage and never makes brash decisions when frustrated, angry, or afraid.

I have already been imagining these ideal gun candidates in several ways my whole life. The police carry guns. I didn't grow up in England, so that makes sense to me. I wish they wouldn't kill so many unarmed people, but that's another rant for another day. The point is that the police are (or should be) going through an extensive background check when applying, are rigorously trained, and are held to an incredibly high standard. Now, if I'm not right about that, I'd prefer to instead not think about it. That's how I can sleep at night, knowing that in America there are so many officers who are allowed to kill people. The idea that if they have to do it, it's because they have exhausted all other options and have ethically followed protocol because they are the experts on making that difficult decision. But my point is it makes sense in my head for them to have guns.

It also makes sense for the military to have guns. I mean, it wouldn't be much of an army if they couldn't quickly extinguish vast amounts of life. Wow.

That was a stiff sentence to type, and again, I am only able to sleep at night by thinking that they will massacre humans as a strategic war effort based on preventing the death of Americans. True or not, it reminds me of every movie I've ever seen that showed a vigorous boot camp and strict training. And, most importantly, a chain of command with no room for decision-making by anyone who is not in a high position. I've heard that if troops are being shot at, they have to ask permission to return fire.[17] It's a far more comforting thought than random civilians having the ability to make terrible decisions with lethal machines. Mainly; civilians who are idiots, short-fused, filled with hate, but have not yet committed a felony, can carry guns. That is just disturbing to me.

That was longwinded, but what I'm trying to get at is that the idea of civilians carrying extremely deadly weapons, designed with the sole purpose of killing living things, is only a comforting thought when imagining grown adults who have their shit together.

An analogy that comes to mind when thinking about the concept of gun control is that of your angry parent telling you to turn down your stereo:

[17] *I just googled it and, while the answer to this is complicated, it is basically not true. I still choose to believe that the decision to pull triggers isn't being made by 18-year-old children who have been found to be too young to make the decision to drink alcohol.*

You don't want to. This song sounds excellent when you crank it up. The bass guitar and kick drum don't sound right if you aren't pushing the speakers a bit. You can't feel the low end if it's too quiet. The extra layered parts in the background will just get lost in the mix if you listen to it too quietly. And yet, your parents bang on your door shouting, "Turn that damn rock n' roll down, or we're taking your stereo away!" They just don't get it.

People who are freaking out about a gun like the AR-15 because it looks aggressive and can shoot as fast as you can pull the trigger, just don't get it. It's cool, man.

What is not cool is dead children. Or dead innocent people of any age. So, it would seem to me that just because something is cool, and you like it, that doesn't outweigh its effects on others. Back to the music analogy for a second. If your parents want the music turned down just because they don't want you to enjoy it, then yeah, that's lame. I'm willing to bet that isn't the actual reason, though. If they want it turned down because your infant sibling is taking a nap in the next room well, then, you need to listen to your music someplace else where it won't disturb others.

I jokingly commented on social media the other day in response to a gun post, of which I was proud. I wrote:

*In my opinion, the perfect gun (so perfect that we could outlaw the rest of them) would be something powerful enough to kill a grizzly bear at close range, accurate enough to shoot a deer from long distances, and so slow to reload that after the shooter kills the first child, the rest of the children in the classroom have time to run to away. I'm saying that the only guns that should be legal and protected by the Second Amendment would be muskets from the late 1700s and my new proposed super-musket. I feel like this compromise would leave everyone equally unhappy.*

I shouldn't make light of a terrible debate and a tragic event, but the point is that there is no way to make everyone happy. You either upset the gun enthusiasts a lot, the victims and their families a lot, or everyone just a little.

# WORKSHEET TIME

Think about whichever political party of the big two you agree with more. What are some stances/opinions/promises that a candidate would need to make from the OTHER SIDE of the aisle to win your vote while staying true to their party's principles?

If you need some ideas, check out ISideWith.com

_____

_____

_____

_____

_____

_____

_____

```
        (
     +(-%$
     `=&<
   #>=(#]
     !<$
     {*%
   @!<$
   \}%%<
   ~*%<
        (
     ~!]
      !
/[%{%%<
```

```
)>*<<_
 ^(|%
  (]
!+(|%
```

# CHAPTER IV

SOUP

ILLUSTRATION BY ERIN MAURICE

Have you ever heard the debate on what makes a sandwich a sandwich, and why isn't a hot dog in a bun considered a sandwich? It's not an original debate, and I'm not trying to take any credit for it. That said, it just occurred to me that I think I might have an original example of something to add to this debate. And if I didn't "discover" this comparison, I'll digress by saying that great minds think alike. Anyways, here it is:

## CEREAL IS SOUP.

After you add the milk, you've made a crème de blé froide. That's French for "cold cream of wheat."

And that's not a stretch, if you ask me. Think about almost any "cream of" soup you buy in a can. None of those ingredients produce a cream texture on their own. Cream of broccoli? There is nothing you can do to broccoli to make a creamy texture, other than ADD cream to it. Broccoli doesn't produce a creamy texture, so I'm not sure why it's called cream OF broccoli and not cream WITH broccoli. I don't make the rules, though, so moving on...

Cream of onion, cream of mushroom, cream of whatever. You have to add cream to something that isn't creamy to make a "cream of" soup. And so, by adding milk to a bowl of grain, you've made a chilled cream of cereal.

Perhaps you eat corn-based cereals. And if you agree with me that it shouldn't be "cream OF," then you should be able to say you eat creamed corn for breakfast.

Sometimes titles are bullshit. Kind of like all those dumb job titles mentioned in chapter one, you don't always know what you're dealing with until you get a good look at it and try a taste. Adding a fancy French name to a boring breakfast is just a way to try and sell you something.

I strongly suggest being skeptical of titles as you encounter them. Everyone is trying to convince you that they are essential and should be paid more.

Everyone is trying to convince you that their product or service is best and that you should pay for it. Don't trust them. Everyone is lying for their benefit.

Hell, I'm a professional author now. Let that sink in. I was paid money to produce a published book. I didn't graduate from college. I've never written anything before. I might not write anything professionally ever again. But for some odd reason, I now have the same job title as Stephen King.

I get that a company might come up with a complicated job title for a position, based on the fact that a lot of people might do very similar things. They need to keep their departments organized, so they end up having a bunch of people who all do almost the same thing, with a bunch of different titles based on the specific work they are doing. Internally, that makes sense. The outside world doesn't care, though.

And if you think that trying to make your title sound complicated is going to impress people, well, unfortunately, you might be right. If it didn't work, no one would be doing it. But it's being done. File my distaste for it under, "how I think the world should work."

How I'd love to see the world labeled would be in the most direct, truthful, transparent, and universal way possible. You'd know exactly what you're buying, who you're hiring, what your responsibilities are, and who you're dealing with. You could get the specific education required to perform the tasks involved in a particular position and then you could easily transition from one company to another. Yeah, perfect world scenario.

The world is far from perfect. Society is full of charlatans. Everyone is looking for an angle. No one plays fair, and that's just the way it is. What we all are trying to do, while simultaneously trying to detect it in others, is that old saying, "fake it until you make it."

At some point, great products, fantastic services, and invaluable talent will rise to the top. However, that is such a select few. Most nouns won't rise to the top. Everything can't be the best.

The great news is that this glass is both half-full and half-empty. While only a select few can rise to the top, just some can be the absolute worst! Take this book for example. I think that no matter how hard I try, this won't be the worst book ever written. It might be close, but I can sleep easy knowing that I probably won't ever hold that title.

Here is some icing on that shit-cake: Even the worst of something can be successful for merely winning the title of "worst."

Okay, try to remember:

Degrees = you know how to pass a lot of tests

Confusing job titles ≠ skill, experience, or education

French words ≠ superior products

Cereal is soup

# WORKSHEET TIME!

What are some of the most misleading titles you've seen for products, services, or positions?

_____

_____

_____

_____

_____

_____

_____

_____

# CHAPTER V

DON'T MIND ME; I'M JUST TRYING
TO LIVE FOREVER

ILLUSTRATION BY ANNIE KASSENS

Alright! You're five chapters in, and you haven't given up yet! This is exciting! By now you've probably picked up on my personality a little. You can see that my writing style is pretty care-free. By just decoding letters on a page, your brain is processing who I might be as a person. That's pretty fascinating to me. You probably don't need to try to do it consciously, but the more I write and the more you read, the more you KNOW me.

I often joke about how I want to live long enough that scientists can import my brain algorithms into a computer so that my surviving friends and family can chat with me whenever they want. Sure, my flesh will be long gone, but 100% of what makes me who I am would still exist and in an interactive form. My current brain wouldn't be living forever, but the interactions that people have with "me" WOULD.

If this were possible, my brain's algorithms could keep writing books, writing music, and giving others advice long after I take a dirt-nap. I guess I like the idea of no one ever missing me, but yet at the same time, I don't want to be forgotten.

I've recently started doing some family tree research. I'll share with you a dead end I've reached. My father's name is Albert. His father's name was John (born Jan, but Americanized when he moved here). His father's name was Bartholomew (born Bartłomiej). His parents were... well, no one alive knows. That's the end of the line.

His parent's lives were probably fascinating, but no one else will probably ever know who they were or anything about them. So, unless Great-Grandpa Bart's conception was immaculate, we know his parents existed, but that's it. It's a safe assumption that (unless he was adopted) his father's last name was Marszałkowski. And if his mother and father were married, she likely took on that surname. But their entire story... a lifetime of adventures... are just gone. The same goes for Bart's wife's family.

I don't want that to happen to me. I don't necessarily want to change the world so much that I'm listed in history books for the next millennia. I do want to be discoverable, though. I feel like that's a pretty humble compromise. I'm not so full of myself that I think anyone SHOULD know who I was, but I'm full of myself just enough to want anyone to be able to. Perhaps writing music, recording podcasts, and writing books will do that. Maybe in a hundred years when they can finally do digital consciousness uploads, they'll be able to scan my books and recordings into their systems and create me_2.0 after-the-fact.

This chapter seems like a good place for me to list some basic info for any future descendants researching me, who have no idea who I was. Most of the dates and other details are probably obtainable from the legal documentation, so I'll omit it here, so I'm not leaving you a list of answers to security questions. Here is a general summary:

I was born in 1982 in Milwaukee, Wisconsin, USA.

I spent most of my youth interested in music, video, mythology, and a variety of other interests that in no way translate into lucrative careers.

I received public education from the Greenfield School District, but I did not do well. Attention Deficient Hyperactive Disorder was still pretty much a new thing back in the '80s, and schools didn't yet offer a variety of learning styles. I (barely) graduated in the year 2000.

I worked a variety of jobs for the next eight years, always picking those that would allow myself time to be in a rock band and free to play shows on Saturday nights.

I was in a collection of terrible bands. I'll list here the ones that I wrote songs in: **Landslide, Orphonic Orchestra, The Bard Adherents, and The Everyday Motive**

I married my wife (Desiree) on December 7th, 2008 after dating for six years.

We bought our first house in the summer of 2010.

## V. DON'T MIND ME; I'M JUST TRYING TO LIVE FOREVER.

Our daughter, Charlotte, was born in the summer of 2015. At the time of me writing this, she is currently two years old, sleeping face down on the living room floor after putting off her morning nap as long as possible.

My weight has been in constant fluctuation, gradually gaining weight over the last twenty years. I am 5'8," and I was around 180lbs at the age of 18. In September of 2012, I weighed 274 lbs. I went super crazy over health stuff for a year, and in October of 2013 I weighed in at 205 lbs for a Brazilian Jiu-Jitsu competition (about ten pounds of water was cut right before the weigh-in, and I was 215 the next day). Ever since then, I've slowly gained most of the weight back. Since I'm not writing this book at the end of my life, I can hopefully declare that the story of my health WILL have a happy ending.

As far as I know, I shouldn't be passing on any genetic flaws besides less than average eyesight, hair that grays early, and possibly my mother's peanut allergy. I think the jury is still out on if my ADHD is something that can be inherited, but if you have that, I'm sorry, that's probably my fault.

My paternal haplogroup is N-M46.

My maternal haplogroup is H.

Desiree's maternal haplogroup is V7.

My heritage and Desiree's heritage are both entirely European. As for which countries, specifically, that's still to be determined (we received some contradicting information from the two different tests we did). But, for now, I can say that we are both MOSTLY of Polish descent. But we are super-euro-mutts, and ALL AMERICAN, BABY!

Here is what 23andme.com tells us our DNA says:

| | John | Desiree |
|---|---|---|
| **Mostly Polish,** but also Lithuanian and Russian | 53.4% | |
| **Mostly Polish,** but also Slovakian, Russian, Hungarian, and Ukrainian | | 64.7% |
| Central Europe, mostly **German** | 12.8% | |
| Central Europe, mostly **Austrian** | | 3.3% |
| The United Kingdom, mostly **Irish** | 11.5% | 15.7% |
| Scandinavian | 1.3% | 0.6% |
| Broadly Northwestern European | 12.7% | 8% |
| Balkan, mostly **Romanian** | | 3.6% |
| Balkan, other | 0.1% | |
| Broadly Southern European | 2.9% | 0.5% |
| Ashkenazi Jewish | | 0.1% |
| Broadly European | 5.2% | 3.4% |

And here is what AncestryDNA.com says:

| | John | Desiree |
|---|---|---|
| East: Polish, Lithuanian, Slovakian, Czech Republic, but specifically Pomerania | 71% | |
| East: All of the above PLUS specifically Pomerania, Slovakia, and Hungary | | 67% |
| Great Britain: England, Scotland, and Wales | 16% | |
| Ireland | 7% | 18% |
| Iberian Peninsula: Spain & Portugal | 3% | |
| West: Belgium, France, Germany, Netherlands, Switzerland, Luxembourg, Liechtenstein | 2% | |
| Scandinavia: Sweden, Norway, and Denmark | 1% | 15% |

As you can see: very different results from different tests. It's hard to say for sure when it comes to countries that border each other since borders change over time (unless it's an island). Take Poland, for example. At different points in time, Poland was huge; it didn't exist and then existed again but much smaller than it originally was. So, when someone says they have Polish heritage, that could very well be modern-day Russia, Germany, Austria, Lithuania, and so on. Countries like the modern-day Czech Republic and Slovakia were once engulfed by the Austrian Empire.

Then there was that whole Ottoman Empire thing, and the Nazis, so you get the point. It's easy to see how some of the differences in these charts can be explained by continually changing man-made borders.

Let me get off of genealogy and bring this back to some shitty life lesson like I've been doing in some of these other chapters.

Here is what we know (because science):

- There are not different races, just one human race.
- If you decide your heritage by where your earliest ancestors came from, rather than your most recent ancestors, then we all share the same heritage, which is 100% modern-day Tanzanian.
- If you decide your ethnicity is where you were born, then most people reading this book are going to identify as American. Never mind all that heritage stuff. All you need is jazz music, baseball, apple pie, and a cowboy hat.

I think there is room for some ethnic/heritage identity that's halfway between those two, but I don't think there is an exact science to it where you get to make statements like "I'm exactly 12.5% Irish."

Also, nationalism is stupid. Being proud that you live on one patch of dirt as opposed to a different patch of dirt is stupid. Thinking that "your" culture is "better" than others is stupid. Being proud of a country (which is a man-made government) which is a country you or your relatives voluntarily left, is stupid.

Maybe this is just an American fascination, as we are a nation of immigrants. I think all this heritage stuff stems from wanting to belong to a group, from wanting to feel like there are people who are "your" people, even if you've never met them. Ethnicity offers both that feeling of being a part of a group, but also a sense of individuality in such a diverse environment.

Ethnicity aside, a family can offer this. A family of ancestors and descendants can be humongous, comprising plenty of people you know extremely well alongside distant cousins you've never met. You all belong because you are "blood." Most people you come across in your life will not be family, and so while you are a part of something huge, you are also unique. However, even family is something of a gray area. There will be people in your family that you don't care for, and there will be friends who are not family that you care for immensely. Does it make sense to deny that bond because you don't share the same great-great-great-great-great-grandparents?

And while it might require giving up a sense of uniqueness from belonging to a specific ethnic group, maybe we should all take comfort in knowing that every human alive today shares the same six-thousandth-great-grandparents from Tanzania.

# WORKSHEET TIME!

What things have you created in your life that could be discovered by your decedents a millennium from now? They might know absolutely nothing about you besides what they learn from your creations. Who will they think you were?

_____

_____

_____

_____

_____

_____

_____

# CHAPTER VI

THE ONLY THING RICH CONSERVATIVES
MIGHT BE GOOD FOR IS FINANCIAL ADVICE

ILLUSTRATION BY SARAH HETRICK

Okay, first thing, regarding the title of this chapter: When I say "Financial Advice," I don't mean "Advice." I mean just learning about what they did to not be poor. Their advice to you might suck because sometimes their opinion is to do something different than what worked for them. Their perspective of the world is different, but it's worth hearing, even if you have to discard most of it.

Here is the second thing regarding the title of the chapter: I realize that some wealthy conservatives are useful for more things than just financial advice. I don't know what those things are; I'm not qualified to speak to that.

The third thing regarding the title of the chapter: all conservatives are not wealthy. All rich people are not conservative. You'll have to go with the stereotypes if you want to enjoy that title. Or don't and keep on not enjoying stuff. I will say this, though: If you are a conservative and poor, you are a confused person.

Okay, moving on.

I've read a handful of books about money that can be described as nothing less than right-wing nutbaggery. I did take away some helpful ideas on how to handle money, though. I have to get this out of the way· I am not rich, and I don't know the long-term effects of what I'm about to recommend, so don't take my word for it.

People who are having money trouble are either:

    a. Spending too much money
       As my father would say "Living the champagne lifestyle on a beer budget."
    b. Not making enough money
       I'm not saying it's your fault that you don't make enough money to cover your family's necessary cost of living... I'm just saying that your income is the problem.
    c. All of the above.

## THERE ARE TWO TRENDY STYLES OF BEING A FRUGAL CHEAPSKATE:

One, which involves zero debt. The other, which embraces reality. There are a lot of passionate debates online about the pros and cons of credit card rewards, low-interest loans, and so on. No one is right or wrong. Many well-off people subscribe to either method.

Here is my advice on budgeting: Make a budget and try to follow it. If you struggle to stick to it, at least make yourself extremely conscious of how much money comes in and goes out. Get yourself to have a firm understanding of what you expect to spend every month versus what you will earn and do everything in your power to spend less money than you make.

Here is my advice on emergency funds: Have an emergency fund. That's obvious, I know. But it clicked for me when I started thinking about it differently.

In the past, I used credit cards for emergencies and lived paycheck to paycheck. If I had an unexpected $700 mechanic bill, it went on a credit card, and I paid as much as I could toward the card each month until it was eventually paid off. I liked this method because the credit card gave me peace of mind for if an emergency happens, I can survive it.

The problem is that having credit card payments in addition to my regular bills prevented me from saving money and was the reason why life was always paycheck to paycheck.

The new perspective I allowed myself to have was this: Be your own bank. Borrow money from yourself. And just like that, it clicked for me. If I borrow money from myself, I don't have to pay interest.

I had just finished reading a book that emphasized the importance of STARTING with an emergency fund of only $1000, so I went with that. The idea was that I was going to get $1000 into my untouched savings account, and

I was going to keep it at $1000 no matter what. And if I had to borrow money from it, I had to pay it back right away to make it $1000 again. It was REALLY hard to get $1000 together, but I went into crisis mode and did everything I could to come up with that cash. The $1000 is still there. I've borrowed during the unexpected but repaid it. I've started putting money into a second savings account ever since paying off the credit cards. I just needed that tiny shift in mental security. Just knowing I had a small little safety net gave me the courage to throw every single penny I could find at our debt. It also helps that my wife has been incredibly career-focused and that we've avoided childcare costs by me staying home with our daughter. Then, for extra cash, I do side-hustling on the weekends like filming weddings, taking photos at events, and selling bad books to suckers.

If you didn't pick up on this by now, I don't think you should borrow any money for almost any reason if you have a balance on any credit cards. Credit card interest sucks way too bad for you to focus on anything else besides paying them off. The zero-debt attitude is an excellent method to get out of debt.

## CREDIT CARDS

Here is my two cents on reward cards:

I don't see the harm in using a credit card for the rewards, so long as you...

- Pay the full balance by the due date, every single month, forever. Setting up autopay can make this a reality.
- Don't put something on a credit card that you can't pay for with cash. You're using the credit card as an extra step to get rewards, not to borrow money before payday. Regularly monitoring your budget makes this easy.
- Don't use a card with an annual fee, unless cash rewards are guaranteed, like to buy things you will continuously need no matter what, such as groceries or gasoline. The card I have that gives me the most cash back does so for grocery stores and gas stations, so it makes the annual fee worth it.

- Don't expect considerable payouts in rewards. At the time of me writing this, my cards get me as low as 2% cash back, which means I have to spend $1000 to get twenty bucks back. It's a better option NOT to pay $1000 if you can help it. You save $1000 instead of $20 that way. It's kind of like coupons. If having the coupon makes you buy something you wouldn't have purchased otherwise, then the coupon isn't saving you money. However, if you had unlimited "2% off ANYTHING from ANYWHERE" coupons, you'd use them, wouldn't you?
- Do not use any credit cards if you don't have the self-control to use them appropriately, regardless of the rewards.
- Behavior > Math.

So, more on that last bullet; This is why I don't laugh off the whole "No debt, no matter what" approach to finance. I think spending money can be a PROBLEM for people. It has been for me in the past. The same way people can have a gambling problem, drug addiction, eating disorder, or what have you. If you are addicted to spending money, it's just not a good idea to put yourself in the position to make bad choices. It's a risky thing. You're taking a significant risk if you don't trust yourself. Better to play it safe than save a little money. Here is a little analogy I thought up:

If you're trying to save money on food, but you are addicted to roulette, DO NOT EAT LUNCH AT THE CASINO'S FREE BUFFET!

It doesn't matter that the buffet is free. It doesn't matter how much money that will save you when you do the math. What you aren't calculating is the risk you're taking that you might make some bad choices by having to walk past the roulette table every day.

I wouldn't let anyone else tell you if borrowing money is in your best interest. That's most likely something you know about yourself more than anyone else. The exception being a person whom with you share a bank account. They can probably give you some solid perspective.

Okay, moving on.

## LOANS

Here is my two cents on loans:

- You lose money the longer you borrow it, but if you borrow money on something that MAKES money or appreciates at a better rate, you come out ahead. If your house appreciates at a rate that is higher than that of your mortgage, you don't need to rush to pay it off. If you have extra money to throw at your principle, you're probably better off to invest that money in the market where it will likely have an even higher rate of return.
    - Reason to not follow this: If you are scared of risks, like your house not appreciating as much as you predict it should; the chance that the market won't steadily grow over time, as it has in the past. The risk that your career could have a low point, where you struggle to make the payments on your loans. If these things keep you up at night, you should probably avoid debt. Know that making money and calculated risk often go hand in hand.
- Credit Union loans almost always have better interest rates than banks, credit cards, or financing directly from a seller.
- It's best to avoid car loans. Your car will only depreciate, so borrowing money for a car is expensive. Cars are the type of thing that is best to save up for and pay in full. I'd say save up as much as you can and then borrow no more than $5,000. But let's be honest: We usually look for a car because we are in NEED of a vehicle, not because we're planning 5-10 years out. So here is my challenge to myself and you: Let's save $75/month from now on, just for the next car that we pay for in cash. That might not be the next car we buy, but it's for the next car we buy without borrowing. Let me explain in too much detail:
    - At the time of writing this, I see that I can buy a specific 2005 car for $4,200. I could also buy a 2015 version of the same model for $12,663. This difference in price tells me that buying

a three-year-old car and then selling it ten years later will cost me $8,463 in depreciation. That's just over $70/month.

- If you are buying a business vehicle, such as a taxi, snow plow, or food truck, your rate of return could potentially be higher than your depreciation and interest, so things like this are the exception. Make sure it's something that is increasing your revenue, and not just something that makes life easier (unless making life easier causes you to have more time, and then you use that time to make more money).

## INVESTING

I only hope that I can get this message to some kids in their early twenties who have a SHIT LOAD of years ahead of them before retirement. The fact that retirement is far away is NOT the reason to put off saving for it. It's precisely the reason to start; you can be lazy as shit about it and end up rich as fuck!

Example time:

A lazy, dumb 18-year-old gets a minimum wage job ($7.25 today) doing something stupid. He makes $15,080/year. He never works a second of overtime. He never gets a second job.

He becomes the first person in US history to be hired and work fifty years for the same employer without ever getting a promotion or a raise of any kind. That's right, the cost of living goes up and the minimum wage doubles in time, but he, for some reason, keeps making $7.25.

He never moves out of his mom's basement. He takes the bus. He eats a lot of spaghetti. Okay, you get the idea. So, this lazy fucker decides to do something as soon as he is hired: He opens up a savings account and has 20% of his paycheck dumped into it every payday. Then, once a year, he buys $3000 worth of mutual funds in a ROTH IRA account. Let's say he gets something like Vanguard Capital Opportunity Fund Investor Shares (VHCOX). He invests $3000/year for the next fifty years. But before you do the math on that, go ahead and look up VHCOX. As of right now, over the last fifteen years, that fund has averaged over a 13% rate of return with the second-largest market crash since the Depression. The risk is low. The reward is high. This lazy piece of shit retires with 11.7 million dollars! And he doesn't have to pay any taxes on it because he already paid the tax before he invested it. He took $150,000 and turned it into $11,700,000 doing almost nothing at all besides living on 80% of his pay.

I'd be curious to see how close my numbers are fifty years from now. I'm only going off the last fifteen years. But if I'm half right, he still has over 5 million dollars. If I'm only 10% right, he's still a millionaire. And this is factoring in all that lazy shit that you are probably not. You probably have some dreams and aspirations. You probably will leave a job for a better job at some point. You'll get out of dead-end positions and get into places with room to grow. You'll see cost-of-living increases. You'll be in a position to invest far more than $3000/year without it destroying your lifestyle. And all it requires is that you're 18 years old.

Oh, shit, I'm sorry. You're not 18, are you? You're probably much, much older than that, and you possibly have crippling student loan debts, car payments, mortgages, and so on. So yes, for you, it would have to be more than $3000 a year. You have less time for compound interest to make you stupid-rich, so even though you'll invest far more, you'll still end up with far less.

18-year-old dude starts at 18, invests $3,000/year, retires with $11.7 million.

A 43-year-old person starts at 43, invests twice as much for half the time, retires with $1.05 million. Better than nothing.

They both invested the same amount of money ($150k) but the one that spread it out over more time made over 10x more.

So, the bad news is you can't go back in time. The good news is you can look up a compound interest calculator online and figure out how much you need to start investing right now to have as much as you need by the time you don't want to work anymore.

That's the other crazy thing about investing. The people who aggressively save for retirement don't retire when they are old and broken. They retire when they don't need income anymore because their investments are paying out more money than they need to live.

I'll end this financial chapter now on the only piece of advice that matters, which is that...

## YOU SHOULDN'T TAKE MY ADVICE

You should take the advice of a financial advisor. Yes, I already mentioned this in a footnote, but it bears repeating.

I recommend a fiduciary. Some financial advisors make more commissions from selling some things rather than others. Fiduciaries will work in your best interest because they get paid more when you make more money. That way you don't need to worry about them recommending something that isn't in your best interest. You want them getting paid based on how wealthy they are making you, not based on what they can talk you into.

It doesn't hurt to take advice from trusted friends and family who are stupid-rich. Just heed this warning: If they try to sell you Whole Life insurance, run.

Oh shit, I should probably say something about...

## INSURANCE

If you have kids who are dependent on you, get a goddamn Term Life insurance policy immediately! The one you (might) get from your employer doesn't count, because if you quit or get fired, you can't keep it! Take your annual salary, multiply it by 10, then get a term policy on yourself for that amount for at least as long as you think your kids won't need financial assistance from you. Do the same thing for your spouse. You don't need life insurance for kids.

Avoid "Whole Life" insurance. There is a lot of debates on the Internet about this, so research it if you're interested in learning more. I'll say this: Whole Life usually pays the agent the highest commissions... so can you believe an agent who is telling you to buy it from them? Term Life is cheap; they make less money on it, so trust them if they recommend it.

Most importantly, plan your financial goals around being self-insured by the time your term policy ends. That means, have enough money and assets that your family doesn't feel the need to murder you in your sleep the night before the policy runs out.

# WORKSHEET TIME!

Ever wonder what your net worth is? It's easy to figure out, but it's not the amount in your bank account.

1.    How much debt do you have in total? This includes student loans, credit cards, car payments, mortgages, and so on. All debt.

      $ _____

2.    Next, add up how much gross money you would have if you sold your assets. What is your house realistically worth? What is the Kelly Blue Book value of your car for a private sale? Add all this up here.

      $ _____

3.    How much money do you have in your 401(k), IRA, HSA, 529, and so on? How much do you have saved and invested?

      $ _____

4.    Now add the answers to questions 2 and 3 together, as well as whatever you have in your checking account. Then take that amount and subtract the answer to question 1. This amount is your net worth.

      $ _____

# CHAPTER VII

"WHAT CAMERA SHOULD I BUY?"

ILLUSTRATION BY ETHAN CHANDLER

Let me start off by saying that I don't hate being asked this question. I love geeking out about gear. I sometimes think I like window-shopping for cameras and lenses more than actually taking photos.

It's also important to mention that from the time of me writing this and printing this book, some information will already be out of date. So, I'm going to do my best to address these topics with as much of a timeless perspective as possible.

## THE PERFECT LENS

It doesn't exist.

The reason many cameras have interchangeable lenses is that having the right glass is about having the right tool for each job. A photographer with an extensive collection of lenses is kind of like a handyman with a vast array of different hardware. The alternative is a camera with a fixed lens being like a guy with a roll of duct tape in one hand and WD40 in the other. Neither is wrong, but it depends on the project.

Another comparison would be like culinary utensils. Some people can cook what they want with one pot and one spoon. Others need an extensive collection of "stuff." Neither is wrong, so long as you have what you need to make the thing you want to make.

So I guess the question to ask yourself before you go shopping is this: "What kind of pictures and/or video do I want to take?"

I like to take pictures of people. Taking pictures of good-looking people is a great way to avoid needing to know a million photo tricks because photos of beautiful people automatically look like beautiful photos to the layman. So, I'm going to address lens qualities for shooting people here.

## SHALLOW DEPTH OF FIELD

This is the official terminology for saying "the subject is in focus, but the background is out of focus." This look is trendy, and I'll tell you why I think it is: Camera phones can't do it very well—YET. I think people are impressed by things that they think they can't do. Kind of like how backflips are impressive to people who can't do backflips. Photos that are hard to take with a cell phone are what usually impresses most people.

You can capture this look comfortably in one of two ways:

- Get a lens with a wide aperture, or
- Get a lens with a large zoom

The aperture is usually referred to as the f-stop. A lens labeled as f/1.2 is going to have an aperture that opens up pretty darn wide. This lets in more light and also creates that shallow depth of field. However, a lens labeled f/5.6 is going to have an aperture that is much narrower.

However, even f/5.6 can look shallow if you are zoomed in enough. There is a mathematical formula for it, but all you need to know is that there is a ratio that will affect the depth of field: the ratio of the distance between the camera, the subject, and the background. For example, if the background is twice as far from the subject as the subject is from the camera, it's likely going to have a shallow depth of field. However, if the camera is twice as far from the subject as the subject is from the background, you're more likely to take a photo where the subject and the background are both in focus.

Having a zoom lens essentially changes the look of the distance between the camera and the subject, so it becomes easier to manipulate the ratio to create a shallow depth of field—even with a narrow aperture.

We can't always back up and zoom in, so it's more convenient to have some wider-angled lenses that have more wide apertures. For example, I have a 20mm f/1.8 lens which I often think looks a little too wide (it makes rooms look bigger than they look in real life). At f/1.8, I can take an excellent shallow depth of field photo in cramped spaces, like an elevator or something like that. I can quickly create that ratio where the wall of the elevator is twice as far from the subject than I am. That's because, with a wide lens, I can get much closer to the subject and still have a lot of the subject in the frame.

Now, the 200mm f/2.8 is going to look shallower than the 20mm f/1.8, because you have the zoom factor in addition to a relatively large aperture. However, 200mm makes it very hard to back up enough in a lot of situations.

## DISTORTIONS/COMPRESSION

I've found 50mm to be a beautiful portrait focal length, but I'd never want to take a portrait of someone's face with the 20mm because wide angles can distort shapes (like making rooms look bigger); wide-angle close-ups of faces often turn a human head into the form of an egg. Just like too much zoom will flatten a shape.

## WHAT EXISTS?

As far as the perfect lens goes, you want something that isn't too wide and isn't too zoomed, with a large aperture. If you're buying a lens that zooms, you'd want a lens that has a vast range of zooming distance, but also as low of an f-stop number as possible.

Here is the dilemma: due to the mechanics of how lenses work, the perfect lens doesn't exist, so it's all about compromising what range you want to give up and how wide-open you need your aperture to be able to get.

I currently think the best zoom lenses you can own would be both of these: The 24-70 f/2.8 and the 70-200 f/2.8. The aperture of f/2.8 is a great compromise. Sure, f/1.2 is better, but you won't find these zoom ranges with that aperture. The same way you will see lenses that zoom from 18mm to 300mm, but they might have f-stops as narrow as f/6.3. A 24-200mm f/2.8 would be excellent, but it doesn't exist because the mechanics don't allow it.

If you're willing to compromise the aperture, even more, the kit lenses that come with most DSLR cameras have a decent range of zoom, such as the 24-105 f/4.

That's just if zooming with the lens is ideal for your situations. If you find that you can almost always "zoom with your feet," then you can get a much sharper looking photo with a prime lens (that is a fixed focal length). That's where you have to worry about being too wide or too zoomed. The 50mm f/1.8 is probably the best dollar-for-dollar value when it comes to lenses. You get a great aperture of f/1.8. 50mm is a pretty normal looking focal distance, too; not too wide or zoomed. On a full-frame camera, it looks pretty similar to what the human eye sees. So as long as you are always able to back up or walk closer, the "nifty fifty" is excellent and cheap, making it the best lens you can buy for as little money as possible.

## THE PERFECT CAMERA BODY

This matters SO MUCH LESS than the lens. I think the two most important aspects of a camera body are the sensor size and the speed. Ask yourself if it matters how fast you need to be able to take pictures and how vital is low light performance.

- Do you need to be able to shoot 16 photos a second, or would three photos a second be acceptable for you?
- Can you spare an extra moment to let auto-focus find a general point of focus, or do you need it to analyze every single tiny section of the frame to see the optimal focus settings in a fraction of a second?
- Do you need to be able to shoot fast-moving subjects in darkness without using a flash, or is that not necessary?

I prefer a large image sensor because it performs better in low light situations than smaller sensors of the same quality. For the work I do, I need to be able to shoot in very dark conditions where I can't always add light. Specifically for video, you want the largest-sized sensor that you can afford. And that's the kicker: A full frame sensor (35mm) is a big jump in price from a crop sensor (smaller than 35mm). You don't NEED this, especially if you can use a flash and you have wider and faster lenses. I know that I went from an APS-C sensor to a full frame, and I can't go back. I'd be willing to go back if the camera tech for low light improves considerably but, for now, I think the perfect camera body is going to have a full frame sensor. However, if your question is, "what is the best camera body I can get for under x-amount of money?" then I'm going to say "Whatever has the fastest processor, most focus points, and the largest sensor that you can afford."

It's also important to point out that your camera body is going to drop in value a lot, and fast. Just like a computer or almost any tech out there, it won't be long before something better comes out, and possibly for less money. If you treat your photography/videography competitively at all (like for business), be ready to buy new bodies every couple of years to stay "relevant." Your lenses, on the other hand, are not going to depreciate as fast or as much. With many cameras, you can keep using your lenses on new bodies. If you buy your glass used, you can usually sell them years later for just as much as you paid. So, lenses should be your significant investment—not bodies.

## ADVICE FOR GETTING INTO PHOTOGRAPHY

Buy the cheapest used DSLR you can find. Don't worry about anything else if you are "new." If you are seriously trying to learn the art of photography and the operation of manual controls, you don't need anything "nice." You can honestly practice composition with your phone camera. You can practice operation of manual settings on the cheapest DSLR out there.

If this isn't what you want to hear, I have a feeling you fall into the next category...

## YOU WANT YOUR PHOTOS TO LOOK BETTER AUTOMATICALLY, AND YOU'RE READY TO THROW MONEY AT THE PROBLEM

As I said in the "Depth of Field" section, photos that look like a phone didn't take them are often the result of a decent camera with decent editing. So sometimes, just owning a good DSLR is enough of a boost in quality to give you a look that you want, which is only slightly better than most phones.

That said, a great photographer will likely out-shoot your DSLR shots with their phone, because they probably understand composition far better than usual. The subject and the composition of the shot matter far more than the capabilities of a camera.

It might be a few years, but you'll get there eventually. However, if you want photos to immediately look A LOT better by doing virtually the same thing you already do with your phone, the bad news is that you can't throw money at that problem, other than just hiring a professional.

You can move up in camera equipment. It won't make your skills any better automatically, but they will look better by using bigger sensors and sharper glass.

That's a little fact that professional photographers like to avoid discussing: A great camera and great lens in "auto" mode is going to take better pictures than a worse camera and a worse lens. You can still take terrible photos with superb gear, but naturally better tools help make a better product.

## TIME FOR COMPARISONS

Owning expensive knives is not needed to mince food, but if you know how to do it, it's a lot easier to dice food with great blades. The quality of the chopping will be improved by sharper knives, rather than by dull knives used by the same chef. If you get the chance to meet Gordon Ramsey and you can only ask him one question, you don't ask him what knives he uses. His knowledge of what to do with knives is more valuable than the brand of the knife he uses. But yes, whatever blades he uses are probably better knives than what you own, and if you bought them, the quality of your mincing would probably improve by 20% or something.

The same concept can be applied toward many comparisons. You don't ask a plumber what kind of wrenches he uses with the idea that if you own those wrenches, you won't need to hire a plumber.

Owning a Fender Stratocaster will not move you closer to a goal of sounding like Jimi Hendrix, but it is going to feel and sound so much better than a cheap Peavey. But if you don't know how to play, the best guitar in the world will still sound bad.

I could keep going, but you get the idea.

So, to wrap this up, if you want to spend money, buy the camera with the largest sensor and the fastest processor you can afford.

# WORKSHEET TIME!

Here is a fun little chart I made to show you how far away the minimum distance your background should be from your subject, based on how far away you are from the subject. To make this list simple, I'm going to use just one camera and one lens at one f-stop: APSC crop-sensor body with a 35mm lens at f/4 (I made the camera and lens settings a cheap option on purpose).

Now ask yourself this: How far away do you like to be from people when you take their picture? How far away from a wall or background should you ask them to stand? (Hint: The answer is shoot as close as you can to frame everyone and ask them to stand as far away from the background as possible).

| Distance of Camera from Subject | Minimum Distance of Subject from Background |
|---|---|
| 4' | > 1' |
| 16' | > 7' (about half) |
| 27' | > 28' (about equal) |
| 52' | > A half-mile |
| > 53' | You are too damn far away from the subject. What the hell are you doing? Everything in your shot will look like a flat field of 2D depthless-ness. |

# KAPITEL ACHT

---

„MUTTER DER GNADE, ICH SPRECHE
KEIN JAPANISCH!"

ILLUSTRATION BY VON WILL SUTTON

Ein berühmtes Zitat von Chris Farley von Saturday Night Live. Es fasst meine Einstellung jedes Mal zusammen, wenn ich versuche, Duolingo zu benutzen und in eine Sackgasse gerate.. Wie ich in den vorherigen Kapiteln gesagt habe, fällt es mir schwer, Dinge zu lernen. Besonders in einem Klassenzimmer. Duolingo gibt mir für ein paar Tage ein gutes Gefühl, aber dann merke ich schnell: Je länger ich es mache, desto schwieriger wird es. Wie Sie sehen, versuche ich Deutsch zu lernen. Wenn Sie fließend Deutsch sprechen, haben Sie festgestellt, dass ich nicht auf Deutsch sondern auf Englisch schreibe. Dann benutze ich den Google Übersetzer, um es in Deutsch zu konvertieren. Ich hoffe, dass die meisten Leser dieses Kapitel einfach überspringen werden, weil sie den Text nicht aus der physischen Kopie des Buchs kopieren und einfügen können. Auf der anderen Seite könnte das Ebook mein Geheimnis lüften; dass dieses Kapitel nur ein Füller ist, sodass das Buch größer aussieht, als es wirklich ist.

Ich werde wahrscheinlich meine entfernte Cousine Djul Marszalkowski fragen, ob sie sich bereit erklärt, dieses Kapitel zuerst zu korrigieren. Sie ist Deutsche, trotz unseres polnischen Namens. Ich bin sehr beeindruckt von ihren zweisprachigen Fähigkeiten. Wir können nicht wirklich verwandt sein, wir haben nur den gleichen Nachnamen, was nicht üblich ist. Ich habe sie auf Facebook gefunden. Sie ist meine Brieffreundin. Sie ist cool.

Sie fragte mich vor kurzem, warum ich Deutsch lernen wollte und ich sagte ihr die Wahrheit: Ich will Rammsteins Texte verstehen. Das ist es. Ich habe keinen anderen Grund, die Sprache zu verstehen. Ich fühle das Gleiche für das Klavier. Ich würde gerne Klavierspielen lernen, aber nur genug, um Billy Joels „Piano Man" auf Partys vorzutragen. Ich würde auch gerne „Roll Out The Barrels" auf einem Akkordeon spielen, aber das war's. Nichts anderes. Ich mag kleine erreichbare Ziele, wenn es um schwierige Herausforderungen geht. Ich denke, vielleicht sollte ich das bei dieser Gewichtsverlust-Sache ebenfalls machen, zum Beispiel der leichteste professionelle Sumo-Ringer der Welt zu werden oder so.

Ich werde jetzt den großartigen Monolog zitieren, den Al Pacino als „Ricky Roma" im Film „Glengarry Glen Ross" 1992 aufgeführt hat.

Ich mache das aus keinem anderen Grund, als dass er ausgezeichnet ist, also nehme ich an, dass er auf Deutsch erstaunlich klingt. Genießen Sie's.

*"Du dumme Scheißfotze.*

*Du, Williamson, ich rede mit dir, Scheißkerl.*

*Du hast mich sechstausend Dollar gekostet. Sechstausend Dollar und einen Cadillac. Was wirst du dagegen tun? Was wirst du dagegen tun, Arschloch?*

*Du bist scheiße. Wo hast du dein Handwerk gelernt, du dumme Scheißfotze, du Idiot?*

*Wer hat dir jemals gesagt, dass du mit Männern arbeiten kannst?*

*Oh, ich werde deinen Job haben, Scheißkopf. Ich werde ins Stadtzentrum gehen, und mich mit Mitch und Murray unterhalten, ich werde zu Lemkin gehen. Es ist mir egal, wessen Neffe du bist, wen du kennst, wessen Schwanz du lutschst, du gehst aus. Ich schwöre dir, du gehst ...*

*Jeder in diesem Büro lebt von seinem Verstand.*

*Du wurdest angestellt, um uns zu helfen. Ist dir das klar? Um uns zu helfen. Nicht um uns zu ficken. Männern zu helfen, die ihren Lebensunterhalt verdienen wollen, du Fee. Du Firmenmann.*

*Ich werde dir noch was sagen, ich hoffe, du hast das Gelenk abgerissen, ich kann deinem Freund hier etwas sagen, das ihm helfen könnte, dich zu fangen.*

*Du solltest die erste Regel lernen die du wissen solltest hättest du auch nur einen Tag gelebt. Öffne niemals deinen Mund, bis du weißt, wie der Hase läuft. Du verficktes Kind."*

# ARBEITSBLATT-ZEIT!

Oh MIST! Dieses Buch interaktiv!

Stimmt; Sie können entweder in das Erlebnis eintauchen, indem Sie dieses Arbeitsblatt ausfüllen, oder Sie können es ignorieren. Wie auch immer, können Sie sich vorstellen, wie kurz dieses Buch aussehen würde, wenn ich Füllstoffe wie diese nicht einbaue? Alles klar, los geht's...

Können Sie zehn deutsche Wörter aus diesem Kapitel auflisten, deren Bedeutung Sie kennen?

_____

_____

_____

_____

_____

_____

_____

```
=!_
{*%
^>[#%
@%
~({*
_>}
```

# CHAPTER IX

WANTING TO WANT WANTING

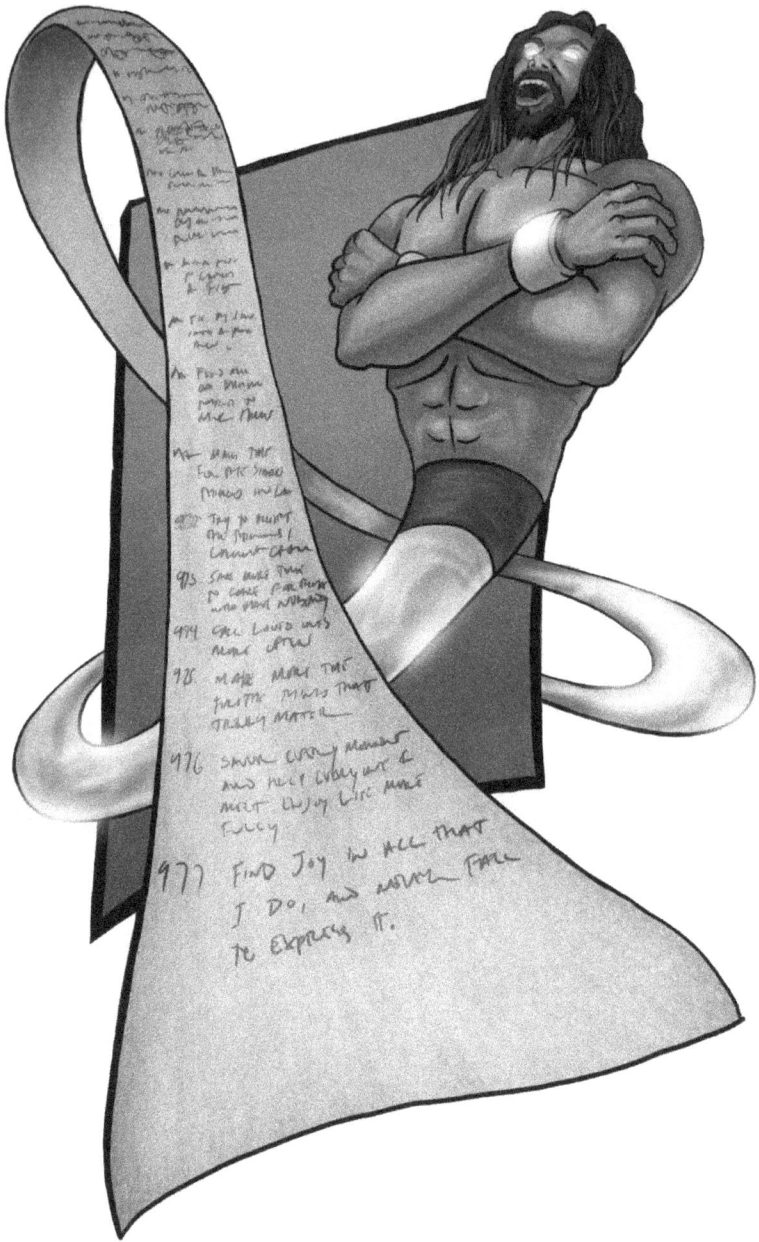

ILLUSTRATION BY KENNETH UZQUIANO

I'm pretty sure life is a nonstop checklist of things to do until you die. Then you don't have to do anything anymore. While that concept seems a little depressing, I think it gives us meaning and happiness. Sometimes that list has things on it we don't want to do, but completing something still gives us satisfaction, and most importantly, it lets us start our next task.

I'm currently working on a pretty basic list.

- Increase the size of my family's rainy-day savings fund
- Get our house cleaned/repaired enough to make it sellable
- Make my gut slightly smaller
- Keep my daughter alive while my wife is at work
- Get more sponsors for my podcast
- Write more songs
- Upgrade my camera gear
- Learn to speak German
- Finish this book

The weird part is trying to imagine what comes next. For example, if I suddenly stumbled into an enormous amount of money, I could solve the rainy-day fund, pay for home repairs, negate the need for podcast sponsors, and then upgrade camera gear all I want. So, suddenly about half of the list is gone... but does that let me focus on the other half twice as hard? No, probably not. I will probably fill up the list again.

I said it's weird to try and imagine what comes next and, to test this, let's pretend I have a magic genie for a second. Now, I am suddenly in shape, I have a ton of song ideas, I speak fluent German, and my book is done, printed, and for sale. So, how does my list fill up again? Or does it? What happens if it doesn't? That's the part I can't imagine.

In this fantasy, all those new songs need to get recorded and rehearsed for some performance, don't they?

BOOM, genie does all of that.

Okay, time to promote it and—

BOOM, done.

Okaaaay... well time to shop for a new house and —

BOOM, we now own our dream home.

Hmm... well, I guess I can take that new camera gear and —

BOOM, I have a full portfolio and all the money I'll ever need.

Wow. Well, time to get in shape so I can—

BOOM, I look like Jason Momoa.

Damn! So, I guess I'll plan a trip to Germany to practice my—

BOOM. Ich bin in Deutschland und spreche Deutsch.

Nice. I guess I'll start my next book then—

BOOM. All future books are written and published.

Well, I guess I now have all the time, energy, and resources in the world to focus on raising my daughter with my wife and—

BOOM. Daughter is raised, educated, and at the top of her career.

WHOA, WHOA, WHOA, SLOW DOWN! Back it up! I don't want this! I don't want everything to be complete. I want to participate in the act of completing things, and I don't want that list to run out.

That's probably the meaning of life, or something similarly anticlimactic.

Now, to be fair, in the genie situation I got to skip the things I didn't want to do. Like, the amount of hard work and plastic surgery required to transform into Jason Momoa is nothing I want to experience. The whole "It's not the destination, it's the journey" thing doesn't work in this scenario. That is not a journey I'd want to experience in the slightest. Sure, the destination is lovely, but it's not worth the trip. I think the route to looking somewhat like Alec Baldwin would be a much more manageable trip, but the destination isn't exactly paradise, either. It's kind of like taking a vacation to a cartel-infested part of Mexico. Sure, it's easy to pay for, but do you even want to go there, when Paris is what you had in mind?

Something like building an adequately-sized savings fund isn't that miserable or that rewarding. Saving a dollar isn't nearly as bad as running a mile. However, a big savings account (full of money you don't spend) isn't as sexy as Aquaman. So, enjoying that journey of saving money is a "meh" journey.

Selling, buying, and moving into a new home is a stressful process. That doesn't necessarily mean I would want to skip it, either. I mean, when it comes to browsing and shopping houses, I enjoy that a lot. I think that applies to most kinds of shopping. I mean, except for grocery shopping, I like buying things.

At the time of my writing this, the podcast doesn't have too many paid sponsors, but it doesn't need any, either. We're past the initial overhead of buying stuff, and the only recurring expense at this point is the beer we drink on each episode. And, let's be serious—we are going to buy beer anyway. Total transparency: Steve buys the beer, and I bought most of the gear and the web stuff. So far I've spent more, but at the rate we're going, Steve is going to end up spending a lot more. So, it would be ideal to get paid a consistent $20 per episode to cover the beer. But, man oh man, it would be nice to eventually make some extra cash only by doing something we would do anyway. That's a journey I definitely will enjoy taking, and I guess I'm not in a hurry to be past it.

Writing music can be hard work, but it's also very therapeutic sometimes. And like all the things mentioned above, there is the satisfaction that comes from completing a task and overcoming its challenges. The same thing goes for writing this book, some kinds of exercise, learning a language—you name it.

I want to want. I often find myself wanting to want wanting. A back that never itches isn't necessarily better than an itchy back that gets scratched. I need to want to have obstacles in my way, not just to be past them.

# WORKSHEET TIME!

If everything on your to-do list was done, what would be next for you?

_____

_____

_____

_____

_____

_____

_____

```
^}#-
{[}=/
  (
|>{%$
 ^>[
@%[<(%
```

# CHAPTER X

DON'T WAKE ME UP; THE DREAM IS BETTER

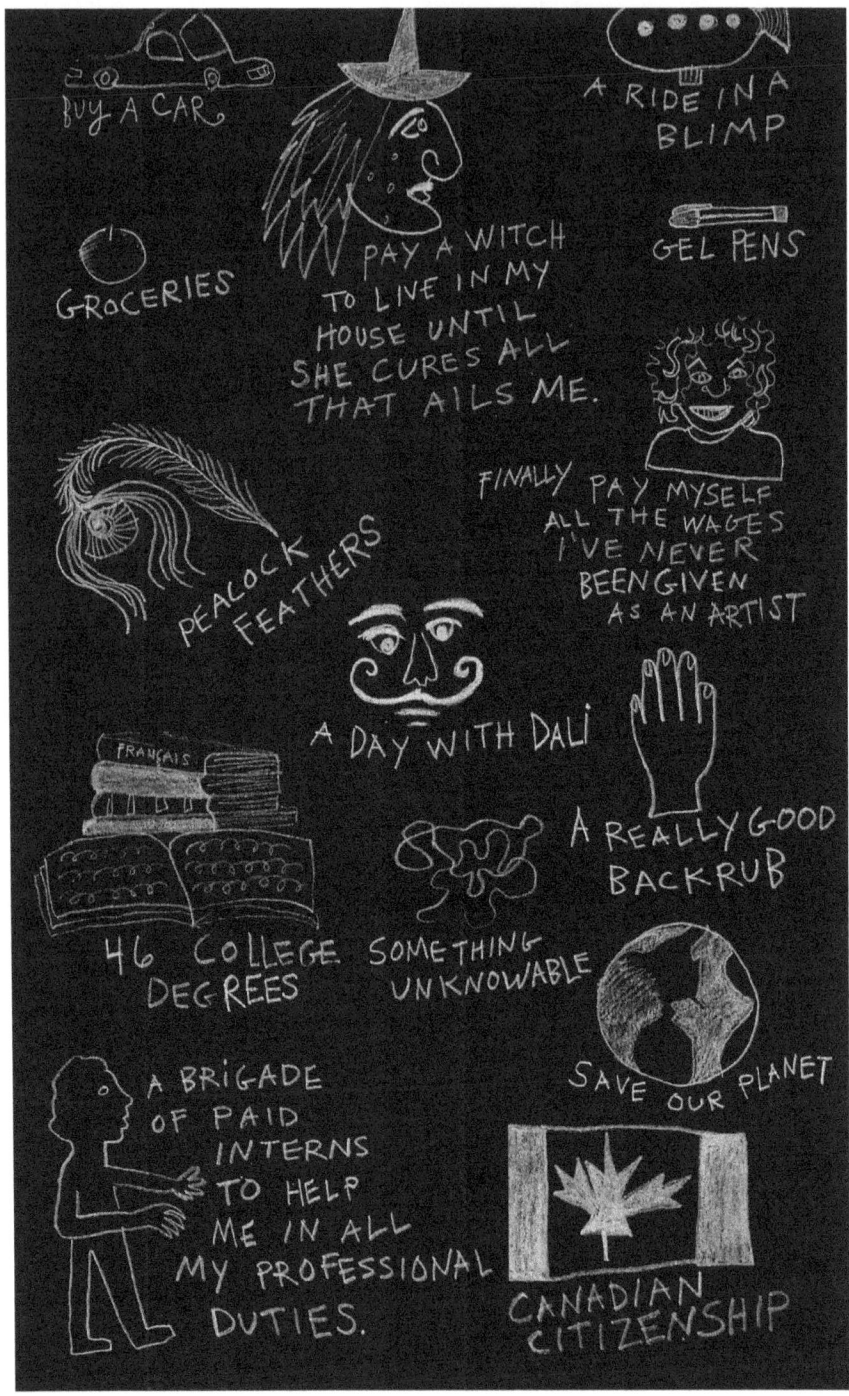

BUY A CAR

A RIDE IN A BLIMP

GROCERIES

PAY A WITCH TO LIVE IN MY HOUSE UNTIL SHE CURES ALL THAT AILS ME.

GEL PENS

PEACOCK FEATHERS

FINALLY PAY MYSELF ALL THE WAGES I'VE NEVER BEEN GIVEN AS AN ARTIST

A DAY WITH DALI

FRANÇAIS

A REALLY GOOD BACKRUB

46 COLLEGE DEGREES

SOMETHING UNKNOWABLE

SAVE OUR PLANET

A BRIGADE OF PAID INTERNS TO HELP ME IN ALL MY PROFESSIONAL DUTIES.

CANADIAN CITIZENSHIP

ILLUSTRATION BY ANJA NOTANJA SIEGER

Do you ever notice when you casually talk with someone about what you'll do with your money after you win the jackpot, some chemical gets released into your brain? I don't know if that's true, I just made that up. It could be a hope thing. It might feel terrific to think about life without any financial concerns.

When my wife and I do that, we always get specific about it, down to what we'd name our charity foundations. We'd talk about what our house would look like and what neighborhood it would be in. We'd talk about fun business venture ideas and how we'd fill our time. Gosh, it feels amazing to remember talking about that.

It's pretty fun to think of things to do with excess. However, I'm pretty surprised by how many people don't consider the basics BEFORE thinking about the surplus.

I asked the following question publicly on Facebook:

## QUESTION: WHAT WOULD YOU DO IF YOU WON THE LOTTERY?

The answer everyone gave was the same thing, which is the freedom of their time. For many people, that meant not working the job they have. Not to say they wouldn't work, but they would fill that time with what they want to do, not because they needed what it pays.

Check out Tristian's fiscally conservative response:

*"I would invest it in large-cap growth stocks, and withdraw 4% of my balance every year. Live the rest of my life on about $50k salary without ever having to work."*

My guess is he would work on something, but he wouldn't "have to" work for money. The second comment was from Mike, who has no plans of being lazy, but wants the freedom to stay busy in the ways that he wants:

*"I'd like to do what we are doing now, but on a bigger scale. A bigger house, more land... but not having to work, so I can teach my boys to hunt, fish, fix cars, and raise animals."*

That sounds like a lot more work than I'd care to do, but I can see how it must be overwhelming to try and cram all of that into two-day weekends, along with relaxing enough to recharge for the next work week of doing something else.

Dawn had a little bit of humor. Depressing, but still a joke...

*"I'd pay off my student loans and have $74 left!"*

I hope she's joking. I know student loans are crippling for many people, but the idea of winning the lottery is to explore the fantasy of having excess. However, payments on such a significant amount would be a relief to no longer need to pay every month. So, even to walk away with only $74 in her pocket still leaves her with a lot more wiggle room in her budget to start building wealth.

Jen wrote an excellent plan, and I think the part that is so amazing about it is that it doesn't take a jackpot to make this kind of thing happen. I mean, winning the lottery makes it happen fast, but over a lifetime this is all realistic:

*"It sounds pretty boring, but I wouldn't want to tell anyone. WI law doesn't allow lottery winners to remain anonymous. So, I would hire a lawyer to advise me; then I'd invest 80% (I would take the slow pay option). With the remaining 20%, I would expand my kitchen and get new floors for our house, which I'd pay off. I'd pay off my student loans too, which would leave us debt-free. Sam could quit his job and work on his pug websites[18] and designs full time. I would write at PBG[19] still because I love it, but I'd also work on a vegan cookbook*

---

[18] *darklordpug.com*

[19] *postsbyghost.com*

*and keep Ecology Runner[20] going. I'd buy everything on my Amazon wishlist, buy some clothes and take some trips (Paris, Montreal, Egypt, Thailand, New Zealand, Alaska). I would probably get a nose job because I hate my nose.[21] Then in the long term, I'd start a sanctuary farm with a staff, yoga classes, and a vegan kitchen. With the payout from investments, we'd start a foundation to help rescue pugs and cats, and we'd continue to run the farm. Oh, and I'd invest in some cool art."*

I'd like to end this chapter with an unoriginal thought regarding lottery tickets: It is a tax on the poor. It is money collected by the government, but people who don't play don't pay. You know who doesn't play? Rich people. It's the poor people with dreams that fund it. And almost everyone loses. It's a tax that only poor people pay, to give welfare to the extreme few who win. Stop playing the lottery, take that money, and invest it in the market. That kind of gambling has much better odds.

---

[20] *ecologyrunner.com*

[21] *Jen's entire face is adorable and she's crazy for wanting to change it.*

# WORKSHEET TIME!

If you suddenly came into $250,000,000 (after taxes), it would be decent of you to donate at least 10% of it to charities in need, right? Which charities would you cut these checks to?

**$250,000** paid to the order of _____

**$500,000** paid to the order of _____

**$750,000** paid to the order of _____

**$1 MILLION** paid to the order of _____

**$5 MILLION** paid to the order of _____

**$7.5 MILLION** paid to the order of _____

**$10 MILLION** paid to the order of _____

**Extra Credit:** Double each amount, divide that by 10,000, and **actually write** and mail all of these checks over the next 12 months.

Example: For the first charity you listed, go to their website, click on donate, get the address, get out your checkbook, and pay this amount... ($250,000 x 2) /10,000 = $50

# CHAPTER XI

---

## I'M NOT A BAD DAD, BUT I'M BAD AT... SOMETHING

ILLUSTRATION BY WILL SUTTON

I've been going through an emotional rollercoaster lately. In a nutshell, I love my daughter, but I feel guilty about my lack of parenting skills.

I get that this is a learning experience that all first-time parents go through. I realize that being a stay-at-home parent is harder work than society would have us believe. However, I can't shake this idea that because I'm not a natural at it, or because I don't love the work aspect of parenting, that maybe I'm a lousy dad.

Let me try and break down what's going on in my head as best I can.

- I love my daughter.
- I love her smile.
- I love her laugh.
- I love when she dances along with TV shows.
- I love when she sneakily tries to stick her foot in my face when I'm watching TV.
- I love how much she loves those coin-operated car things at the mall.
- I love watching her face on the zoo train.
- I love how much she loves her mama.
- I love her hugs and kisses.
- I love how she points to things she wants and yells "ME!"
- I love her giggle that she uses in place of the word "yes." Example:
  "Do you want water?"
  "No!"
  "Do you want milk?"
  "hehe"
  "Can you say MILK?"
  "ME! ME! ME!"
- I love taking her for long car rides to nowhere, because she prefers taking naps in her car seat and she is endlessly entertained by just looking out the window when she's awake.
- I love how she says "Hello!" and "Bye-Bye!" to every single person in the grocery store. Everyone.

- I love how she steals mushrooms and black olives off my pizza while I'm eating.
- I love the smell of her breath after she eats graham crackers.
- I love that she loves Barbra Streisand and the film Hello Dolly.
- I love that she is literally the result of how much I love her mother. Like a living trophy that my wife digs me.
- I love everything about her.

So here comes the next set of bullets, and they are NOT things I don't love about her. They are things I don't love about myself.

- I don't like what happens to me when she cries.
- My anxiety goes through the roof.
- I become furious at my lack of control over the situation.
- I don't like that I feel like I need to physically limit her when we are out in public, the way you would want to leash a dog or something.
- I don't like the conflict in my head that I feel when I have to force myself to switch whatever I'm focusing on when she wants my attention.
- I hate the guilt I feel for enjoying the parts of the day that don't require parenting, like when she is asleep or when she is playing with toys independently.

So, in conclusion to my lists, I feel like I'm a good dad, but I'm not the best parent.

My sister asked me how I liked being a stay-at-home dad shortly after my wife's maternity leave ended, and I replied with my honest opinion:

*"It's not my favorite job I've ever had. I'd quit if that were an option. It's not. At least I can't be fired. I love my kid, though. It's way better than raising someone else's kid, I imagine. I wish I could out-earn my wife so she could stay home, but that's not realistic. So, it is what it is."*

My sister seemed a little disturbed by this response. I don't think she understood what I was saying.

- I wasn't saying I was incapable of doing it.
- I wasn't saying that I didn't like spending time with my daughter.
- I wasn't saying I was miserable.

I was saying that I wish I could be meeting clients, editing, replying to sales inquiries, balancing my books, updating my website, or virtually any other task that wasn't troubleshooting a crying baby.

Fast forward a year, and it's the same situation. Charlotte is a little more independent when she plays with toys. She sometimes watches TV without my participation for small blocks of time. I'm able to reply to a sales lead mid-day, occasionally. I don't hate my job of being a stay-at-home dad, but I do daydream about a future where I could "go to work" while she is in school.

So, over the last couple of years, I've been asked a couple of dozen times by random people if we are planning on having more kids. I always responded honestly with, "I feel like one is probably enough," but it's a lot more complicated than that.

My wife knows that she wants a second child.

The fact that my wife wants a second child makes me want a second child. The way I never would have considered getting a cat, but my wife wanting a cat made me want a cat.

However, my wife has said that she wouldn't want to have a second child if I don't want to. That's a peculiar position for me to be in because the desire I have for a second child is almost entirely influenced by her hope to have a second child. She wants to avoid me becoming a parent to a second child if I don't want a second child... the same way I want to prevent denying her a second child.

I told her that I'd like to have a second child because she wants one. She didn't love that. I made this comparison:

*"It's like if you ask me what I want for dinner, and I'm thinking in my head that I don't know, but tacos are always a safe bet. Then you say you want lasagna and then I think: yeah, that's a good idea. I probably would have got tacos if it was just up to me, but I could go for lasagna if that's what you want."*

I think what's happening is that we are both worried about resentment. Like, if we had a second kid and I resented her for it. Or if I said "pass," then she would resent me. We've both said that we wouldn't begrudge the other. That puts us back to square one.

This sent me on an inward journey to try and figure out if I want a second child at all or if I only want to make my wife happy.

**Cons:**

- My dreams of "going to work" when the kid is in school would reset back to zero, and it'd be a solid 5-6 more years before I get to be career-focused again
- We'll have to double our savings, and the budget will get tighter
- I could be potentially doubling my anxiety for the foreseeable future

**Pros:**

- My heart will increase in size by 33%

That single pro is pretty compelling. Let me explain how I came up with such a specific number.

When my wife and I first discussed having a first child, I remember having this fear that I wouldn't be able to love a child enough, because I loved my wife with all of my heart. I was afraid a child would steal some of that love. Like if my wife loved me less, because she loves our kid more. To my surprise, it wasn't like that. I remember my heart doubling in size. All the love I had for my wife just multiplied, and now I was in love with two ladies with all of my heart.

Because of that, I know that's what would happen with a second child. My heart would increase in size again. I would love that child with what feels like everything I have to give. And just like my first born, they would be worth any "con" I can come up with. I'd spend the rest of my life thinking "I'm so glad we chose you."

I'd also probably spend the rest of my life wondering what silence sounds like.

...and why everything is sticky.

# WORKSHEET TIME!

## WHY IS THE BABY CRYING?

Absolutely No Reason
Bored
Freaked Out
Gas
Hungry

Important Phone Call
It Is Tired
Overstimulated
Pee
Poop

Thirsty
To Break You
You Are Tired

```
N M K P T Y N U U N H N V S D B L N U C
G B M P D N A F T J O W M D E R O B J D
N L Y D P K R K Y R D E R I T S I T I V
Z G F E E F X O U T I Y N Z A P Q D L S
J H F V S H F A V T S K L E L R D O B Y
D H E C N S E K T S I R R U U N H L I Q
X W L I C X Y X L F D O I L M G R J I G
B L K G X U E R W J N W P H I L E J W V
N A H W R Y O F G Y D E G L T T S H H J
V I E B Z H G R L N P M C Z S A C V M X
O I D E R I T E R A U O Y Q R U G P C A
C I M P O R T A N T P H O N E C A L L R
D Y C I H U N K O P U E E P V F A U Z Y
S H A P L A V E Z Z H V D E O H S Y Q Q
V I K O W X D D G R Q A R P X I R P D B
L P S M F K Q O U H T H N T T J V S O C
I B I N E S T U Z W W U C P L Y G T X P
A M M C F E W T W O T O B R E A K Y O U
J S G W O J V O F E G Y F Y S E U D T G
L T O I B T E V V Z G O X D S Q N A G U
```

# CHAPTER XII

WHAT'S THE POINT OF ANYTHING?

PHOTO BY JENNIFER JANVIERE

## XII. WHAT'S THE POINT OF ANYTHING?

This chapter isn't as much of a downer as its title suggests. I've briefly touched on this subject in other sections, but I want to focus on it for a moment. Mainly, because I need to remind myself why I do almost any of the things I do.

There is an ocean of podcasts, books, music, videos, photography, and other art out there right now—a never-ending sea of people rambling on about whatever. Some people are good at it. Most people are not. No one has enough time to sort through them all. It's one big mess of everyone talking at the same time and virtually no one listening. Almost everything I do feels like it falls into that category of, "You could probably be reading/listening/watching something else right now instead." That's why I sometimes get that pesky question echoing around in my head: What's the point of any of this?

As I've said before, I make things. I start shit. I'm a planner. I'm not always the best executor, but I love everything that comes before it. When I manage to break through that initial warm and cozy place of "planning" and succeed at the actual execution, it's because of (usually) one reason: I love making shit.

I have a handful of favorite books in my life, but I never enjoyed reading much when I was younger. The reason was that I always thought that I'd prefer to be spending the time telling my own story instead of reading someone else's.

I listened to a lot of music, but I never loved watching musicians stand on a stage and play because I always thought about how much more I'd enjoy being the one in the spotlight.

I'd prefer to put paint on canvas than go to the museum.

I'd preferably take photos than look at pictures.

And in any situation where I was observing, it was mostly to be inspired or learn how to be better at what I did myself.

111

I've had a theory about this, which is part of the reason for my low self-esteem, and that is that I'm merely a douchebag that wants to be the center of attention. Internally, I'm screaming, "Don't look at them and what they've done! LOOK AT ME!" I cringe inwardly at this perception of myself. I want to believe that my "need to create" stems from something more respectable, but it probably doesn't. Perhaps it doesn't work for anyone, come to think of it.

A sometimes-wise old sage I know named Shane once ranted about a topic that hit home for me. I'll never forget it. This is not a real quote, because I'm writing what I think I remember him saying:

- If you love writing music, write it down and lock it up.
- If you love playing music, play it with the door shut.
- If you love jamming with your friends, stay in the basement.
- If you like to record albums, don't show them to anyone.
- If you like playing on a stage because you want the lights & sound, then don't invite anyone to the concert or hope that anyone shows up.
- But if anything about that doesn't sit right with you, you have to accept that you are doing this (at least in part) for attention, admiration, respect, status, legacy, and/or money.

Yeah, he didn't say all of that. He likely only mentioned the part about "playing music with the door shut." But the above is the message I took away from it. That is that you should stop kidding yourself that you are a creative person for everyone but yourself. You are a creative person for everyone else and especially, above all else, for yourself.

Okay, fast-forward to now (Happy New Year, 2018!) and apply this to the two dumbest projects I have going on right now:

- Who Are We To Podcast?
- Buy My Book

Both of these things seem incredibly self-indulgent. They appear to function almost exclusively for attention. Why should anyone pay attention? Hint: It's practically one-sided.

- I want people to listen to me.
- I want people to think I am interesting.
- I want people to perceive me as respectable.
- I want men to wish they were me.
- I want women to be jealous of my wife.
- I want people to believe I'm an authority on what I do.
- I want my descendants to remember me.

I think the one difference—and this is big—is that both projects I designed with a not-quite-nihilistic foundation. Specifically, I do not NEED anyone to listen to my podcast. I do not NEED you to read this book. I created them because I want them to exist. I am doing them because they are activities that I'm going to do, regardless. I am going to drink beer and talk too much with Steve and our friends. Yeah, it's also a podcast in case anyone else gives a shit. I'm going to journal out all of these ideas I'm having. If you want to read them, you can.

It does get a little tricky, though. With the podcast, I do want enough listeners to create a tiny amount of demand for really cheap ads, so that we can pay for the beer. With the book, I want to sell enough copies to cover the costs involved in making it. Beyond its expense, any profits would justify the point I made in the book's introduction. So, with both of these things, they are slightly driven by money, but only enough to fund their existence.

So, while there are plenty of reasons to not do something, there are some excellently rewarding reasons to try:

- Attention
- Admiration
- Respect
- Status
- Legacy
- Money

# WORKSHEET TIME!

What is something you do for attention?

What is something you are admired for or would like to be admired for?

What is something you do that deserves respect?

What is your status in society?

How will you be remembered?

If you answered with the same thing for more than one question, is there any way you can monetize it (if you haven't already)?

# CHAPTER XIII

JOHN'S TIPS FOR LIFE

ILLUSTRATION BY CHRISTY HALL WATSON

# 1. DO NOT BUY TOMATO-BASED FOOD IN A CAN.

Spaghetti sauce in a can? Get the fuck out of here. However, canned tomatoes, if you cook them down for a long time, might be acceptable.

## 2. BUY ONE ROLL OF WEIRD-COLORED TOILET PAPER.

It's like a warning roll. If you get down to the pink roll, it's time to buy more of the white immediately.

## 3. DO NOT BUY WHITE UNDERWEAR.

This has got to be one of the worst ideas ever. I mean, it makes sense for athletic socks, because who cares if you get a little discoloration with those? Throw a little bleach in the wash, and they are fine. But seriously… what good can come from white underwear?

## 4. GO BOWLING.

Like, seriously. If you are bored or looking for something to do with your significant other, friends, or even by yourself, go bowling. You don't need to be good at it. I'm freaking terrible at it. It's still fun. You can take kids. You can drink if you're of age. You can eat comfort food. It's not that expensive if you go on the right days at the right times.

Here is another life-tip, related to bowling: buy a ball and get it drilled for your dumb-shaped paw. It costs a lot less than you think it will. Never bought a new ball and had it custom-drilled for your fingers? Take a wild guess what that might cost. $200? Nah, man. The drilling is freaking free when you buy a new ball from the pro-shop. How much does a new ball cost? Fancy ones are costly, but I bought a very basic one on clearance for $20.

I can say with full confidence that you could buy a cheap ball at full price for under $50. This is worth every penny if you have short and fat sausage fingers like me.

## 5.  THE (WISCONSIN) BRANDY OLD FASHIONED IS THE BEST COCKTAIL.

That might seem like an opinion, but it's not. Okay, I guess it is. But, it's a good opinion. Here is why:

Some people like hard liquor that burns your chest like you just drank poison. While you sit there contemplating your mortality, you're probably asking yourself, "Why am I drinking fire on purpose?"

That's why I switched to brandy. It's 80-proof wine. So, if you're making a Brandy Old Fashioned, you muddle sugar, cherries, and orange together (yum!) then sprinkle on some bitters, dump in 1-2 ounces of brandy over ice, and pour Sprite or whatever to fill your glass. Garnish with more cherries or orange, if you're fancy.

I mean, come on. How can that taste bad? Fruit, sugar, soda, and hardcore-wine. If you don't like cocktails because they don't "taste good" then it's time to switch to the Wisconsin Old Fashioned. And the Wisconsin part is important. In other parts of the country, they might not add fruit or brandy, because they want it to taste worse for some reason. The drink didn't originally use brandy, but when it showed up in the Midwest, all the sauerkraut-eating motherfuckers were like, "This drink is good, but it would be even better with brandy."

# WORKSHEET TIME!

## BANDS I LIKE

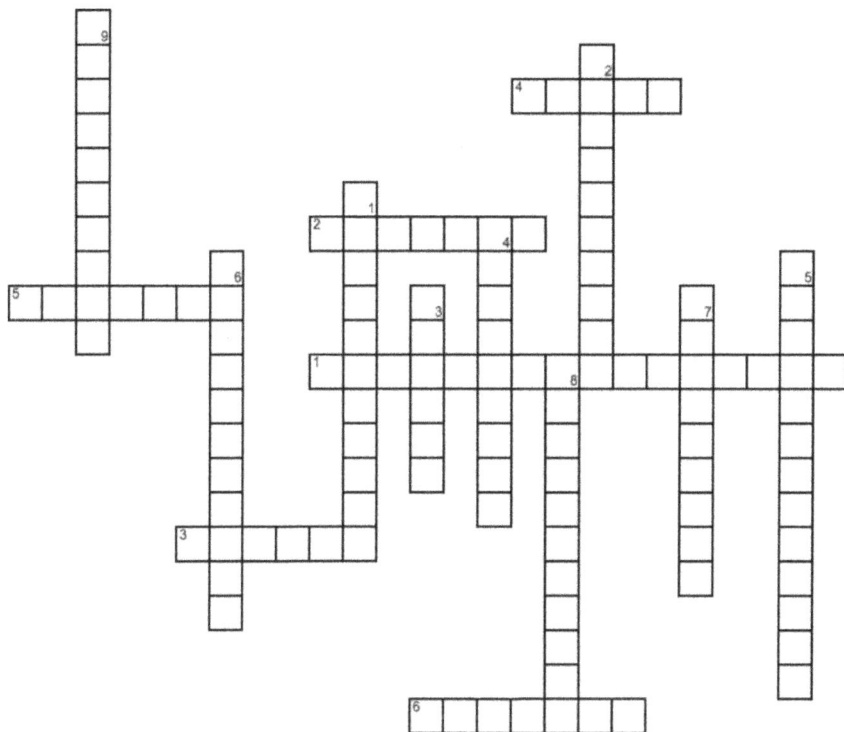

ACROSS

1. No one likes this band but me.
2. RIP in 1994
3. I liked this band a lot in the '90s, but not so much after that.
4. Loved this band my whole life.
5. Bad city; good band.
6. Mother of God!

DOWN

1. I liked this band since 1995
2. I like girls who rock, fight, and break up the band
3. I like family bands of mostly sisters
4. Just the Tarja era
5. I know these guys, kind of
6. Better as a one-man-band
7. Das ist gut
8. Far too long for snakes

```
{*(]
@>>-
 (]
<>{
~>[{*
{*%
=><%_
```

# CHAPTER XIV

---

YOU CAN DO IT! OR MAYBE YOU CAN'T.
EITHER WAY.

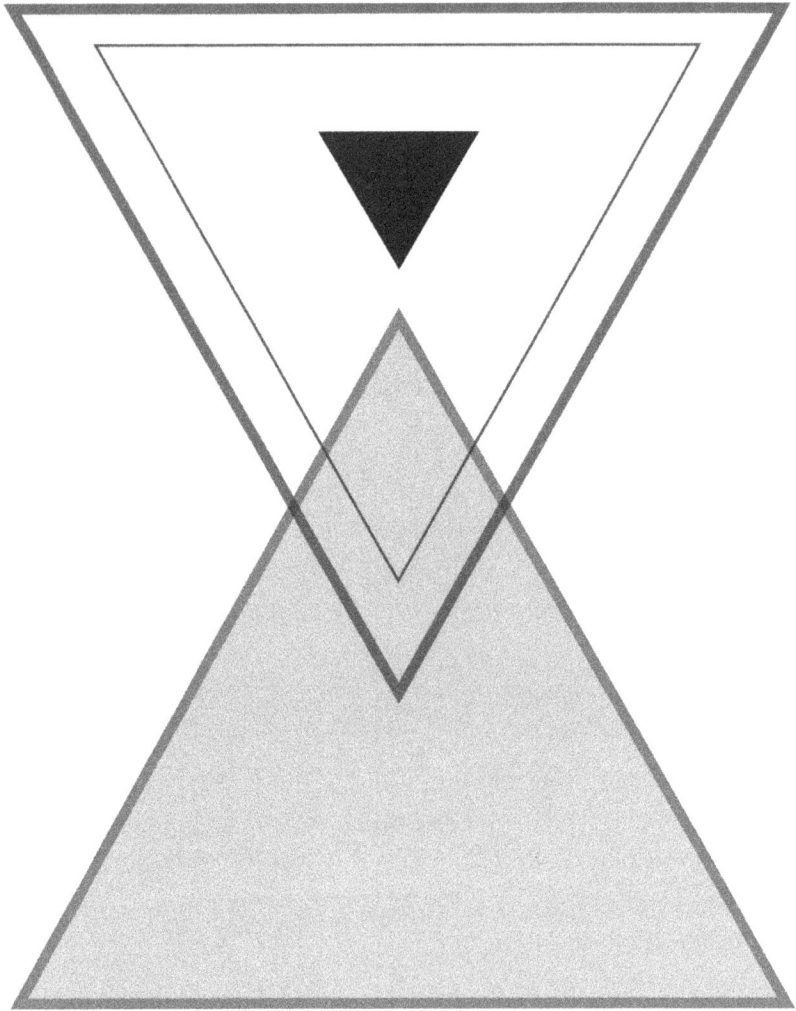

ILLUSTRATION BY MATTHEW KOPF

I want to take a moment to talk a little bit about motivation, self-control, willpower, and all those other admirable qualities that I lack and have no authority for which to speak. And yet, here I am, doing whatever the hell I want because it's my book. This is what you signed up for.

I'm a firm believer in the concept that one good idea is not a good idea for everyone. Example: Jogging is good for people. False. Jogging is good for people for which good results come from jogging. This is not everyone. Someone with bad knees should probably not jog. I don't have a source for this. I pulled it out of my ass. It seems like common sense. If jogging brings some people more trouble than good, then a blanket statement such as "Jogging is good for people" is not true. Jogging is good for some people. Or most people. But not people in general. There are exceptions, such as "Breathing is good for living humans." Kind of hard to disagree with that. But you get my point, I hope.

Without even getting into the commercialization of fitness and nutrition, there are plenty of reasons for people to be skeptical about fad diets and exercise plans. Simply put, what works well for one person may not work well for another. While this is not some original breakthrough thought, here is my two extra cents:

I think the mistake people make with this thought process is that if "plan A" yields "result A" for "person A" then "plan A" will yield "result A" for "person B." However, plan A might only work slightly well for person B. And that's because, due to a variety of reasons, shit is just harder for person B. Plan B might be the best option for person B, but even that might be a worse experience than person A's.

And so person B tries plan A and finds that it works even worse for them than plan B did. They don't go back the plan B, because relative to person A's experience, that wasn't working very well either. And so they go on this journey of trying plans C through Z, feeling like a complete failure the whole time, and possibly giving up on having any plan at all.

123

I kind of think this is where I am, mentally, right now. I'm on a journey to find that perfect plan (convinced there is an effortless way to get everything I want with limited obstacles) when, deep down, I already know that I am person J and plan J is harder than I want it to be. All to reach "goal J," which should, but probably doesn't, resemble result J.

What is goal J? It's a lot of things. That's a lot to unpack. It's incredibly specific to me, which is why it's a J-goal and not the same goal as everyone else. But let's be vague about it and say "better mental and physical health" so that it resembles yours and everyone else's goals.

So anyways, it's taken a long time of experimenting to figure out what plan J is. Plan J is a very long list of things, for which I've only unlocked a few items. Here is what I've opened so far from plan J:

- Permanently eliminating things works well.
- Temporarily removing things does more harm than good.
- Remove the ability to make bad choices in the moment. Instead, make the right decisions in preparation for situations, out of the moment.
- Accountability to others is an effective motivator.
- Light competition has proven to be effective; so long as it's light enough that losing doesn't kill the motivation.
- Repetition is crucial, but there needs to be guilt-free access back to the wagon if I fall off.
- Quantity is more important than quality.
- And the list keeps going with hundreds of things I haven't unlocked yet.

Plan J is perfect for me because I'm person J. The problem is sticking to plan J is hard for J people. Person A encounters some mild obstacles with plan A, but more or less plan A fits comfortably into an A-life because those A-holes are good at shit.

Plan J, on the other hand, is continuously at war with a J-life. And that's why statements like "it's not a diet, it's a lifestyle change" kind of gets under my skin. Yeah, it's a lifestyle change, but certain aspects of it kind of suck, and those parts are things we don't want to do. Person A is over there saying some bullshit like "sure, plan A is hard, but the rewards are so worth it!" but person A has never been a J, and vice-versa… so we make all these assumptions about what is hard and what isn't.

That's precisely why this whole argument is full of shit. I have NO IDEA what is hard and what is easy for an A-person. I have no idea why an A-plan works so well for them. I have no idea why an A-plan leads directly to the perfect A-life. All I know and can assume is that it's easy for them and hard for me— OR—that they work hard and I'm a lazy sack of shit.

Or some gray area in the middle.

Okay, let me dive into those bullet points a little more in-depth while I still have your attention on the subject.

Permanently eliminating things works well.

This is because making the right decisions becomes a lot easier when you only have to decide between "Yes" or "No." If you cut red meat out of your diet, then you have one task, which is don't eat red meat. If you screw up, it's because you broke one obvious rule, not because you got tripped up on a variety of good/bad choices. In summary, it turns the challenging tests into true or false questions, which is like 100% easier than a multiple-choice question and infinitely more manageable than a fill-in-the-blank.

Temporarily eliminating things does more harm than good.

Every good thing I've ever done that brought me real results have been something I've stopped. And when I stopped, I lost all my progress. Every habit I have is not something I told myself I could stop doing after a certain amount of time.

Remove the ability to make bad choices in the moment. Instead, make the right decisions in preparation for situations, out of the moment.

Going back to my true-or-false analogy, not every question on every test is going to be true or false. Sometimes you can't avoid having to figure out an answer on the spot. So I kind of look at making choices in advance like cheating on that test by writing down all your answers on a notecard or something. An example would be measuring out serving sizes of prepared food in advance when you are not hungry, so you don't have to decide how much is a correct amount while your stomach is gurgling.

Accountability to others is an effective motivator.

This could be to one person that you respect and want to impress, or it could be to a group of people. Either way, "doing it for yourself" doesn't seem to cut it for some reason. You have a million goals to accomplish the things you want to achieve, but even though it's all based in what you want, for some strange reason you need other people to want you to do these things. And you want these people to acknowledge your success. It is what it is. If you're a J, that's how you roll.

Light competition has proven to be effective, so long as it's light enough that losing doesn't kill the motivation.

I'm not a competitive person. I don't like sports, so I find it strange that competition helps me in this category. I think the reason is it intensifies the accountability to others. Instead of other people saying, "Oh, cool, good for you, I guess," they are instead far more engaged with my results.

Repetition is essential, but there needs to be a guilt-free access back to the wagon if I fall off.

Practice makes perfect, or whatever that 28-day myth says about repetition and habits. What I think is more important is giving yourself a way to get back on the wagon and do it while feeling pride and not shame. I often keep making good choices because I'm proud of my good choices. I stop making the right choices when I've made a wrong choice because now I'm a person who makes terrible decisions. It's a weird momentum thing with me. I eat well when I eat well, but I can't make myself eat well when I didn't eat well. I can go for a walk when I've gone for a walk every day this week. I can't go for a walk when I missed a day this week.

Just writing this out makes me want to tell myself "knock that shit off!" but I've got some psychological issues when it comes to this. So, in short, doing stuff daily is essential. But what's more important is finding out how to keep the momentum going so I can coast through those moments when I fall off the wagon and get back on the wagon feeling like I have my shit together.

Quantity is more important than quality.

When a diet says "eat as much ____ as you like" I've already figured out how to cheat its system. A perfect example is all those 0-point items in Weight Watchers. I can get fat off of those. That's why with things like "low carb" diets, I still have to pay attention to calories in/out. Over the years, I've figured out that certain foods do not make weight loss any easier or harder. It's just about burning more calories than I take in. I could probably lose weight on a canola oil diet if I strictly counted calories. It's also important to note that quantity > quality ≠ portion control. That's because portion control is something I will readily screw up unless I'm already eliminating my ability to make decisions at the moment by planning.

In conclusion, this is some hard shit. It's not easy. I'm not doing a good job of it, so far. I'll try to work on it. Writing all this out was therapeutic for me to reflect on what I need to do.

Just thought that in case you could relate to some of this, you'd know that you're not alone. I often feel alone. I hope you're out there, J-people.

# WORKSHEET TIME

- What does "plan YOU" look like?

- What makes "goal YOU" so unique?

- Do you think that "results YOU" from "plan YOU" will resemble "goal YOU?"

- What makes "person YOU" different from "Person A?"

- What aspects of "plan YOU" are going to be harder or easier than other plans?

# CHAPTER XV

THE CHAPTER AFTER THIS ONE WAS
WRITTEN BY STEVE KEILLER

PHOTO-DIGITAL-WHATEVER BY JOHN MARSZALKOWSKI

This chapter, as well as the next, is a little unorthodox. By now you've figured out that this book does whatever the hell it wants to, so let's get to it.

This chapter is an introduction to the following chapter. It was written by my good friend and colleague, Steve Keiller.

Why is the book suddenly switching authors for a single chapter? Is it so that he can reiterate the book's thesis with his findings? Did we collaborate on research? Do we have a common goal to educate the reader with a universal message?

No.

Steve asked me if he could write a chapter in my book. I said yes. I never asked him what it would be about. I never asked him what his reasons were. I just said yes.

I assume he has something he needs to say, but it's something that only warrants a single chapter and not an entire book. Or perhaps he's heard me talk about this book and its message at great length, and feels he has something to add to it.

Perhaps.

I'd wage my bets that he thinks it would be cool to write a chapter in a published book. That is something I get. If you read my introduction, you know that one of the purposes of this book is to make something tangible to send out into the world that has my stink on it. Steve would like to rub his scent on one chapter, and that is something I'm happy to help him do.

So, let me say a few words about Steve so you can paint a picture in your mind of who is about to start talking to you.

Steve and I grew up in the same city. We're slightly different in age, but we did go to the same high school together for a couple of years. I didn't know him then, but we had friends in common.

Steve had long black hair and wore metal band shirts. I had long brown hair and wore grunge band shirts. He was in a metal band. I was in a grunge band. I crossed his path a couple of times in the halls and tried to avoid eye contact because I thought he was an intimidating-looking motherfucker. I was cooking partners with his future wife in my foods class. That's about all I knew about him at the time.

Years later we would start a project with a mutual friend (Jim) to go to a different neighborhood every week and make YouTube videos of ourselves getting drunk at different dive bars. That was fun.

After a year of filming and editing dumb videos, I asked Steve if he'd be willing to help me film weddings if I started a wedding video business. He said yes. We went out and bought matching cameras, and we've been making wedding videos ever since.

About half a year ago, we resurrected the soul of our project of documenting ourselves drinking by creating a podcast where we shoot the shit and drink beer. This time, it's with microphones instead of cameras (we do have a camera for Facebook live, but it's just a phone, so that doesn't count).

The podcast has been a lot of fun because we get to be ourselves, talk about whatever we want to talk about, forget about making any clients happy and, of course, drink a large variety of local craft beers.

In doing the podcast, Steve and I realized that we have some strong (and sometimes entertaining) opinions about this crazy dumpster fire called life. That was the inspiration for this book.

Specifically, that I have stuff that I want to say. I'm going to say it. I'm going to put it out there for the public to consume if they want to. And then, in some hidden corner of a box marked "free" in a bookstore no one shops at, I will live on forever.

Now seems like a good time to chime in and give a warning.

After writing most of this chapter, I have since had a chance to read Steve's chapter. It is very different from the rest of this book. It's very... "adult." Not that this book is for kids, but while most of the book is a "PG-13," Steve's chapter is a hard "R" rating. I feel compelled to give you that warning.

Sorry, Steve. I just pictured my mother's reaction when she reads it, and I had to warn her. Unless she skipped over this chapter; then she deserves the shock.

Alright, people. I now present to you the man who has been inspired to create ridiculous content in the same way I have.

Ladies and Gentlemen...

Mr. Steven Keiller...

```
         (
]*>}+$
/+!_
{*%
&}({![
=>[%
```

# CHAPTER XVI

DIFFERENT CRAP FROM A DIFFERENT
"WRITER"

CHAPTER WRITTEN BY
STEVEN KEILLER

SCULPTURE BY JAMES RICHARD LITTLETON

Johnny didn't write this chapter. Johnny didn't ask for this chapter. Johnny had no idea what this chapter would be about. I don't even know why Johnny let me write this chapter. Hell, Johnny probably didn't even read this whole chapter.

Johnny probably already stopped reading.

On with this prologue.

When Johnny told me he was writing a book, a little part of me died. It's not that I wished him ill in his endeavor; I was kicking myself for never doing it. I had always wanted to be a writer. Ever since I was old enough to devour my first Stephen King book, I knew that's what I wanted to do. I even paid attention in all of my high school English classes. But I never got past the crippling procrastination that jerks like me suffer.

I've read some pretty good advice from other authors I admire. They all suggest one writes, writes, and writes some more. One can't be a writer if one doesn't write. I tried many times, only to scrap whatever nonsense my brain would puke out before it had a chance to be anything. Maybe it was fear or ambivalence in my own words. Perhaps I never really had anything to say. Whatever the case, it never happened. But since I committed to a chapter for this money grab, I had to make it happen.

I don't think I typed "fuck" yet.

Fuck!

Here are some brief and fucking pointless stories with no plot or anything of value. Each one, ribbed, and shorter than the next, for your pleasure.

## - FREDDY -

Freddy was flying high. He had just started a week of vacation, flipped a car for some easy cash, and had no commitments or plans. He couldn't stop smiling. Or thinking about the woman he just had lunch with... and dessert. Adventure seemed to be right around every corner. It was the height of summer, and it wasn't even humid. Everything was bathed in a surreal orangish glow as he pedaled home in the early evening. He was riding off into the sunset. He hadn't had a day like this in months. Everything was perfect.

Freddy arrived home about 7 pm and enjoyed a smoke as he surveyed his recently-cleaned garage with everything in its right place. He stubbed it out as he headed in, careful to put the butt in the ash can instead of just throwing it into the yard. There wasn't even any long and drawn-out conversations with the neighbors about some bullshit, just friendly waves. Grabbing a shower beer from the fridge, he headed to the bathroom. Even though he just got laid, Freddy was feeling so good, he watched some porn and rubbed one out. His phone buzzed as he stepped into the shower. Nothing like the cold water in late July to wash off the stank.

So fresh and so clean. He started the task of his maintenance. His mood was so good even that was enjoyable. Nothing like a fresh razor to teach that unsightly body hair a lesson. A dab here, a drop there and a generous dusting later, Freddy was ready for action. He finally looked at his phone on the way out of the bathroom.

He saw a message from one of his closest friends, Bill. Bill had an invite to a soft opening at what was hyped to be the best place in town. Freddy realized he hadn't eaten since lunch and the hunger hit him hard. What luck that he should get invited to this new place? But for Freddy, there is always time to meet up for a drink first.

Why wait? He grabbed road beer as he whistled and walked out to his car.

After stopping at a nearby bar for a beer, Freddy and Bill walked over to the new joint. The outside of the place didn't look ready to open. The landscaping wasn't finished, and various pieces of equipment and supplies were strewn about. But that didn't matter; what counted was on the inside. The place specialized in food and beer pairings. Nothing could be better for Freddy. He was animated as he told Bill about his day and wasn't looking at where he was going.

"Watch out for...!"

Bill yelled too late.

Freddy tripped on a crack in the sidewalk and lost his balance. Instead of falling straight down, he struggled to keep upright. His arms were flailing away, and he overcorrected. He started to fall toward the small unfinished lawn. The battle with gravity was lost, and he went down. An old U-channel post cemented into the ground had been cut off instead of removed and stuck up a foot above the ground. Freddy's hands landed on either side of the post, but his momentum couldn't be stopped.

The post entered his left temporal bone and made a sound like someone breaking a dozen hard-boiled eggs. The post traveled through his brain and exited the top of his head before his friend could even finish his sentence. Freddy's mouth was agape, and his eyes were still open. Brain matter, blood, and skull fragments stuck to the top of the pole and his face.

Bill was frozen. He could not look away from the mess that used to be his friend. Spinal reflexes caused Freddy's corpse to move. Fingers twitched slowly and added to the horror. Onlookers started to gather, and the sounds of sirens were close. An unfortunate position to be in, Bill had a front row seat for Freddy's angel lust. Seeing the dark circle slowly form on his shorts was the last straw for Bill. He tried to get some distance before it came out but puked on Freddy's shoes.

## - ULYSSA -

"What a dirty bitch."

Ulyssa said to herself as she left work.

"Why does she always have to be a hard-ass about everything? We sell booze and shit. It's not important! It's bullshit! Who gives a fuck if that pissant fucking bar didn't get their crap today! It's not my fault they called me last minute! Fuck the numbers! Now I gotta drive out to the middle of nowhere and waste my time to appease our corporate masters. Fucking bullshit."

She was yelling now as she drove down the road.

"Fuck! Thanks for ruining my Friday you fucking cunt rag! I'd like to see you take these orders out! You approved it for them, bitch! I hope you drown on that old man's cum you sun bleached, gold digging, fake-tittied slut!"

She sighed.

"Dammit."

She was breathing a little more comfortably now. Sometimes you have to scream at the thought of someone. No real malice intended. She picked up her phone to call her sister. She would have a sympathetic ear. Maybe she could meet her for dinner. Ulyssa always enjoyed swapping horror stories about work with her older sister. It was amazing how the incompetence could run amok.

Her sister didn't answer the phone. She decided to text her. She was pretty good at it. Never taking her eyes off the road for more than 3 seconds at a time. Plus, there was barely any traffic out there. It seemed like she always hit the wrong letters now. She laughed at her autocorrects as she looked down to concentrate on the task at hand fully.

Suddenly the air was forced out of her, and white surrounded her. The phone went flying, the text never sent. Her head slammed into the door that was smashing inwards and was pushing her body to the center console, pinning her against it. The door kept coming and crushed her ribs. The car went spinning through the intersection toward the light pole. Hitting the curb, the driver's side of the car was now in the air as it started to flip.

The rolling crushed the roof in as it headed toward the retaining wall where it came to rest. The impact with the wall was enough to crush the roof into the passenger compartment. This gave the car a wedge shape like one of those ridiculous Matchbox knockoffs. The impact pinned Ulyssa under the dash. She didn't feel the broken neck or the terror of taking her last breaths.

The truck had hit her going about 50 as she ran the red light.

## - CHARLIE -

He saw her in the corner as soon as he walked through the door. He couldn't take his eyes off her. Memories of anything this beautiful failed to rise. Maybe it was the way the light fell on her. Perhaps it was that smile. He did not know this feeling. He wasn't sure he liked this feeling. Never one to be so bold, he slowly walked over to her.

He gathered the nerve to speak to her. He started softly with a shake in his voice. But she was sweet and kind. And a little cruel. She let him stumble along for as long as it took. But he finally got it out.

It only took one soft touch of his fingertips for him to know this was love. Not wanting to ruin it, he tried to keep her there as long as he could. But other customers kept getting in the way. He had to get her out of there. He wondered what his wife would think. Then he decided he didn't care.

Things went so well; she was coming to his home. He wondered where he would take her. Where there would be some privacy; peace and quiet. He couldn't wait to get his hands all over her. They would make magic together. They would be an inimitable couple.

Wholly engrossed with her, he didn't hear his wife come home. He didn't hear her open the door to the back room. His wife stood akimbo with her jaws wide open. She couldn't believe what she was seeing. Charlie was sweating as he touched her in ways he had never touched his wife. She wished she didn't hear it. He was making soft unintelligible noises as he writhed in ecstasy with her.

Anger was quickly building as her eyes shot daggers over his back to her. She was rummaging in her purse for something now. Charlie sensed something and turned around.

He started to apologize instantly. But in his head, he thought it was best to get caught right away and get it over with. He didn't like to hide things, and he couldn't refuse this new one.

He said,

"I'm sorry I bought another synth, baby."

## - KILLER -

Steve woke up in the middle of the night again. He headed downstairs for a drink of water. He tripped on the dog that was following him down. Steve fell down the stairs and snapped his neck.

The dog was ok.

An epilogue seems like a thing that should be here.

I'll leave you not with words of praise for Johnny. Nor thanks for buying this book. Nary deep thoughts about the crap you just skimmed over. No. I'll leave you with an untitled short story, not unlike the ones you just read, that I wrote in 1st or 2nd grade. There is a reason parents save all this crap.

I once saw a jogging puppy dog, and I thought I only imagined it. But I wasn't. So, I took a picture of it. I went home and showed the picture to everyone. I took it to the president. He said,

"It's a miracle!"

Then he said,

"You could be rich and famous if you show it to the guy that hosts Lifestyles of the Rich and Famous."

So I did. And boy, I had a giant swimming pool and ten million dollars. Boy, he was right. I could get rich and famous all at the same time.

The End

# WORKSHEET TIME!

Hey, this is John writing again. Let's give a big hand for Steve!

On a scale of one to five (one being "not at all" and five being "absolutely"), how would you rate the following questions?

_____ Did you enjoy chapter 16?

_____ Are you likely to recommend chapter 16 to someone?

_____ Are you likely to buy a book that is entirely this style of writing?

_____ Do you agree with the following statement?
"This chapter is NOT offensive to me."

_____ What is your total from the above four questions?

If your number is below 12, we apologize for your experience but thank you for trying something new. Enjoy church on Sunday!

If your number is exactly 12, then can we say how impressed we are with your level of indifference? Nice job, nihilist!

If your number is above 12, please consider sending Steve a few words of encouragement to write his book. You can contact Steve c/o Barf-Bag Publishing's contact information on page iv.

# CHAPTER XVII

FIFTY MENTIONS OF FIFTH DIMENSIONS

ILLUSTRATION BY WILLIAM SUTTON

I was asked to write this chapter by Ryan Irons in exchange for some money. So, now this is happening. Written almost entirely to annoy my wife\*, let me now share with you my obsession with the concepts of higher dimensions.

Let me start off by saying that the subject of higher dimensions has been written about by some of the smartest fuckers ever to lecture a university quantum physics course. I am in no way qualified to write about this, but that is also the exact reason you should read what I'm about to write. You and I are morons compared to them, and I'm more qualified to describe it in our native language of idiot-ese.

If, however, you want it explained to you "correctly," then I highly recommend the book, "Imagining the Tenth Dimension: A New Way of Thinking About Time and Space" by Rob Bryanton. Have I read this book? Absolutely not. Have I watched his YouTube video promoting his book? You bet your ass I did! And I'm at a point where I think I can loosely understand it now.

Before you do that, search the web for videos of Carl Sagan explaining flatlanders on an old episode of "Cosmos." Sagan was a master of teaching complicated things so that a child could understand it, and without sounding condescending.

After you've watched these two videos, you will understand everything or more than I do on the subject. But, since you probably didn't do that, I'll now reiterate what I find so fascinating about them.

## THERE ARE PATTERNS!

One of the things that elementary math has taught us all is that once we figure out a pattern of something, we can accurately tell where that thing is going to end up. I remember this math equation from first grade:

---

*\*My wife is so sick of this shit. I seriously talked about it for over a year, wrote a song about it, and would bring up the topic at parties. She would literally leave the room.*

What is the fifth number in this pattern?

1, 4, 2, 5?

The answer is "3" because the repeating pattern is +3 followed by -2.

Start with 1...

+3 = 4

-2 = 2

+3 = 5

-2 = 3

I have no memory of how you solve this shit when it's more complicated, but with something simple like this, we can observe the pattern and then test it.

That's what is exciting about imagining a hypercube, like a tesseract. We can see a discernible pattern in the observable dimensions below.

That pattern is this: Duplicate, then connect all points at right angles.

There can only be a point starting with zero dimensions. It has no length, height, width—nothing. The position represents a location. But when you duplicate it (create another point) and then connect those two points, you have a line. That line has length, so it is one-dimensional.

Then you take that line and duplicate it. Now you have two lines, both connecting two points each. You connect the points from one line to the points on the other line (at right angles), and you have a square. The square has length and width, so it is two-dimensional.

You take the square and duplicate it, so now you have two squares. Connect the four points from one square to the matching four points on the other square (at right angles), and now you have a cube with length, width, depth, and that brings us to the ever-so-familiar third dimension.

So, we have this pattern, and we can make a pretty educated guess about what happens when we apply it to the next dimension to create a 4D cube. Any cube above the third dimension is considered a hypercube, and a fourth-dimensional one is accurately called a tesseract. We take the 3D cube that has eight points, and we duplicate it, then we connect those eight points to the new cube's eight points. But, here is the kicker: to stick with the pattern, we join them at right-angles through the fourth dimension. We can't imagine what that looks like, because we live in the third dimension and it's all we know. However, we can believe a representative distortion!

The same way we can draw a 2D drawing of a cube, and know it represents a 3D cube, we can make a 3D model that represents a tesseract. And we can use more patterns to prove it!

If we took a transparent glass cube and shined a light on it (from a 45° or 135° angle) casting a shadow on the wall, that 2D shadow would distort the 90° angles to look like 45° and 135° angles. But, when looking at it, you would know that those 45°s and 135°s represented 90°s. The pattern we observe is that we can take a dimensional shape and see its shadow in the dimensions below it.

So, just like the pattern of 0D points to 1D lines to 2D squares to 3D cubes, we can look at the model backward with shadows and see the cube cast the shadow of a square (but the light has to be perfect at a right angle). You can take a square piece of paper (that is almost 2D), and if you shine a light on it right, you'll see a line. A line shouldn't have an observable width, but neither should the 2D paper, so you get the idea. And you could do the same thing with a string representing a line and see a tiny little shadow that represents a dot. Again, the string has a small bit of width, so the shadow point has a small bit of width. Both the line and the point should be unobservable, technically.

Okay, so, if we can go back with this pattern, then we should be able to take it forward into the fourth dimension, which is why we know that we can distort the 3D angles so that they represent 4D right-angles. Don't worry—that should sound fucked up. We can't imagine that. We can try. We should try. But it's not going to happen. It's still fun to try. So, one of the things my wife is sick of is my search for a 3D model of a tesseract or, more accurately, a 3D model of a tesseract's shadow.

## THE FOURTH DIMENSION IS REAL

Assuming everyone is on board with acknowledging the fourth dimension as time or duration, we can keep moving forward (no pun intended) into the darkness of hyper-shit-we-can't-see.

It's easy to look back in time and see our lives four-dimensionally. We see a straight line from our birth up into our current moment. Every moment we've lived seems to line up one after the other on a timeline. It takes a little imagination to think of ourselves four-dimensionally, but I like to think of it as a filmstrip.

Each frame is one right after the other. We live in a single frame all the time, but the frames whip past so fast it feels like we exist in motion—but we don't. We are just a single frame at a time. Unlike a projector hurling 24 frames a second onto the screen, we live an infinite number of frames in every fraction of each second. So, our 4D life is somewhat easy to imagine as a long filmstrip. A seemingly perfect straight line, moving from point A to point B.

What we can't see is the end of our lives, since we haven't gotten there yet. But we know we will. It happens to absolutely everyone with no exceptions in the history of the world. We all die eventually. We know that will happen. It's fate.

No, I don't believe in fate, but yes, I do. Death is everyone's fate. You can't avoid it, no matter what. I don't think how or when you die would be set in stone, but then again, I do. After all, after you do pass, your survivors will remember your life and see its entirety (in their minds) from start to finish.

As we are currently in a single frame of our life's filmstrip, this means there is at least a little film still ahead of us. Is it fate? We know it exists, we just can't see what it looks like yet.

Because we can easily imagine our 3D selves moving along the 4D filmstrip of our lives, it's not that hard to imagine a fold in the fourth dimension, pushing us to an alternate reality.

Yeah, from this point on it starts to sound more and more like...

## SCIENCE-FICTION BULLSHIT

I'd love to see the face of a flat-earther flying in a jet (going in a seemingly straight line) the moment they arrive back where they started without ever turning left or right. It would be mind-blowing if you thought the earth was flat. You magically show up again where you started. It's not mind-blowing if you can imagine the planet being round. But if we view our 4D lives the way flat-earthers consider the shape of the earth, then it would seem like magic to all of a sudden arrive at a different point in our life or, more interestingly, an alternate existence.

I'm going to rip off the Möbius strip example, as I can't think of an original version of this. Picture an extremely flat bug walking along a long and thin strip of paper. You twist it one time and connect the edges. The insect keeps walking along in a seemingly straight line, but at one point it is walking on the other side of the paper and then eventually ending up back where it started. Since this bug and the paper's surface seem relatively flat, the insect might not know that it's traveling through a bend in the third dimension.

If the 4D filmstrip of our lives was to bend through the fifth dimension, would we even notice? Nope. Would it seem like magic if we found ourselves in an upside-down reality or back in time? Yup.

## WHY I WON'T SHUT UP ABOUT THE FIFTH DIMENSION

Now, it just gets weirder and weirder as you work your way up to the ninth and tenth dimensions, so I like to kind of "hang out" in the fifth dimension debate. That's where the fun stuff is, like the idea that your reality could have been (or could still be) as cool as Forrest Gump's. An alternate reality, but a reality nonetheless. Maybe a reality you could "get to," somehow.

The more common way of looking at the fifth dimension is like a tree with many branches or a path with many forks. We might often wonder what our lives would have been like if we had done something different in the past. Because our 4D experience appears to be a straight line from birth to death, what we can't see in the fourth dimension is all the forks in the road along the way. All the choices we made, that others made, and things outside of our control, sent us on a crazy maze of rights and lefts and an almost infinite number of forks in the road. The straight line from birth to death isn't straight at all, because the only reality we know is the one with the paths we took. We can make assumptions about what would have been down those other paths, but we can't see them. Not in 3D. Not even in 4D. However, in 5D, we can.

It's kind of like those sports playoff brackets. If your team wins this game, they will go against this other team. However, if they lose, then they will go against a different team. Or they'll be eliminated.

Looking at your life in 5D would be sort of like looking at a playoff bracket of your life.

You could see all of the possibilities of what is in store for you, starting from a single point of origin, and ending with an almost infinite number of endings. Yes, no matter what, it ends with you dying, but did you check-out as a retired brain-surgeon at the age of 107, or did you die in a childhood accident? Did you die of cancer in your Paris villa, or were you blindsided by a drunk driver in Detroit on your way home from the night shift? There is just a limitless number of life paths. They are all genuine, you can imagine what they might be, but you can only see the way you've taken so far. This kind of ties back into my theory of fate. Yes, we know our destiny is death, but the nature of how we die, and the path we take to get to that specific death, is not predetermined. One could argue that all of the possibilities might already be decided, but because of free will, we will play a part in determining on which path we finish.

I remember once having the thought that if Zeus and the other Greek gods were real, the oracles would exist in a 4D reality because in ancient Greek mythology everyone's fate was predetermined. There was nothing you could do to change it. If you learned of your destiny and tried to alter it, you'd be ignoring the fact that it was your fate to discover your future, and it was fate that you try and change your destiny, and the outcome would still be the same fate. In Greek mythology, there was no fifth dimension. There couldn't be, because there were no paths. No forks in the road. Every choice that seemed like it might be wasn't. Those choices were predetermined and just gave the illusion of choice.

Being raised Christian, I was often told something that seemed contradictory but could have a fifth-dimensional explanation. I was told that there isn't fate and that we have free will. The option to do good or to sin. Yet, God had a plan and knew what decisions we'd make. How could we make our own choices if God already knew what they would be?

The answer was if Zeus existed in a 4D universe, then Yahweh must operate in a 5D realm. A realm where we are free to choose whatever fate we decide, but all of the almost limitless options were already spelled out in a predetermined plan. The idea was that God would already know because he would know all of the possible outcomes, but not which path you would take. This theory of mine would later be found to be void because Yahweh was supposedly omniscient so, therefore, if he were looking at his 5D map of your life, he would have to know which path you are going to take. And so, the free will contradiction debate continues. In the end, trying to lump ancient gods into quantum theory dimensions doesn't make sense, unless it's Zeus. Zeus fits perfectly in the fourth.

The idea of some other culture's fortune-tellers (not Greek oracles) "seeing" through the fifth dimension seems like it would make sense, as the future is supposedly never set in stone. "Beware the Ides of March" was a warning. In a fate-based reality, what would be the point of cautioning Caesar? There would be no avoiding his fate. Unless the soothsayer gets off on making people uncomfortable, it implies Caesar's outcome is still pending.

Okay, so to be clear, I'm not saying that real deities exist in higher unobservable dimensions, but I'm stating that it's an exciting concept with which to fantasize. What's really fun to think about is this:

## WHERE ARE WE GOING NEXT?

If we can remember our past fourth-dimensionally (the line of history from our birth to our current position on our timeline), we can either attempt to imagine our future in 4D or 5D. I think we already do this, to an extent, but being conscious of which dimension you are visualizing is essential. Here is why: You are either looking at the path you are already planning to take, or you are looking at your options.

I don't know who coined this concept, but have you ever heard that you should write down where you want to be and then backtrack the steps needed to get to it? For example; if you're going to win the lottery, you would have to buy a ticket before you can win. So now you know a step you have to take to get there. It doesn't mean you will win, but it's still something that you can add to your "to-do" list. Anyways, I think of this as 4D thinking. You have decided what you want, and now you are going to try to negotiate the obstacles of choice so that you can hit as close to your target as possible. I think that this way of thinking is suitable for most types of goal setting.

Slightly different is 5D thinking. "Someday, if I'm ever rich, I'll blah blah blah." You know it's possible that you'll end up wealthy. You also know it's possible that you'll die penniless. Regardless of what you want to happen, and the steps you take, you know these are possibilities. They aren't equal chance possibilities. Your decisions, the decisions of others, and random chance are going to affect the probability of where you end up.

I think that it's healthy to think about your future, both in 4D and in 5D, and to acknowledge which way you are viewing it. It's good to set goals, know where you want to be and how you want to get there, but it's also good to think about all the possibilities involved if you don't stay the course. I think it's healthy to have vague ideas of where you'd like to be.

*"I might move to Maryland and work my way up the corporate ladder for a weapons manufacturer... or move to Tibet to study Buddhism. I haven't decided. Both are possibilities."*

I think this is just fine. You're looking at your future from a five-dimensional point of view. There are almost-limitless options ahead, and that is exciting! However, if you let the chips fall where they may, you might not necessarily be fond of the path you end up on. Can you complain to anyone when you made almost no efforts to end up in a place you wanted to be? This is why it's good to mix both 4D and 5D thinking.

A quote from my friend Kenneth Uzquiano:

*"A friend of mine said it best: "Should is a dirty word." I hold that little quote dear. "Should" presumes a destiny. That there is a particular way that our lives were supposed to be. The "should" lives only in our minds. We allow it to presume itself as the default and can feel everything from slight annoyance to severe depression when it fails to match reality. The should was only ever a hope, a prayer.*

*Big or small, these unrealized "shoulds" build. Clearing them is a lifetime's worth of work, but you'll never realize your path carrying so much weight."*

I realize this isn't groundbreaking. The idea of thinking about what you want to happen in your future, versus what might happen, is not some new idea I thought of. I like to think about it in the context of dimensions of time, the dimensional space above it, and how one moves through the other. What I wouldn't recommend doing too much is looking at your life and how it could have been, versus how it could still be. Reflecting on what your life might be like now, had different things occurred in the past, is what I'd call 6D thinking. It's interesting, but not productive.

## A QUICK EXPLANATION OF 6D THROUGH 10D.
(This Is Some Star Trek Shit)

## 6D

If you can fold the fourth dimension through the fifth dimension to get to a different point in your life, then you can fold the fifth dimension through the sixth to get to a different possible outcome caused by a different origin. A terrible example would be the movie Back To The Future: Part 2. Remember how 2015 Biff stole the almanac and gave it to 1955 Biff? Then, 1985 Biff became Donald Trump? Well, Marty and Doc leave 2015 and go to 1985, but this is after Biff has altered the timeline by giving the almanac to 1955 Biff, so the 1985 that they go to is the changed one. They end up taking the long way to solving this problem. They go back to 1955, prevent young Biff from getting it, then almost move ahead to 1985 where Biff is a little bitch. The movie ends with them getting sidetracked on another adventure.

I say they took a long way because the time machine lets them fold through the fifth dimension to get to other points in time and alternate possibilities. However, if the DeLorean was able to fold through the sixth dimension, then they could have just moved to a position in a different timeline where Biff didn't fuck shit up. They could have just moved from the everything-is-fine-2015-timeline directly to the everything-is-fine-'85-timeline. That analog-looking flux capacitor might have only been able to fuck with the fifth dimension, though.

I hope that explains the sixth dimension a little. In summary, imagine other possibilities in the future affected by a different past, not future opportunities that are still obtainable from your current position in your current timeline.

## 7D

The seventh dimension is taking the entire sixth dimension (which is everything that ever happened or could have happened in our universe) and viewing that as a single point. This means that having a second point to connect would require a second infinite universe that came into existence in a different way than our own. What that line is, is a measurement of differences between the two endless universe points. That single line represents a single variable, such as the value of gravity. If the line represents the amount of gravity from smallest to largest, then the two points could be positioned on the line to show the difference in value. You, however, can't place every infinite universe point on this line, because some universes have the same amount of gravity as ours. To measure them you'd need to move in a new direction off the path. By adding the new variable, that 7D line just changed its shape. The same way connecting a new line to a 1D line makes it 2D, adding a new variable to the 7D line has now made it...

## 8D

So now you have this "shape" which shows the relationships between infinite universes of different origins and how similar or different they are. I find it easier to think of the eighth dimension as more of a chart of information.

At this point, you can see that the pattern is repeating itself. The same way the fifth dimension can fold through the sixth, the eighth can move through the space above it, which is...

## 9D

The same way the sixth-dimensional area for which the fifth dimension folds through is viewed as a single point to move forward, that also happens with the ninth. What IS that point? It's messed up, that's what it is. It's trying to imagine everything that ever was and will be, mixed with everything that it wasn't and won't. It's an infinite number of starting points connected to an endless amount of other never-ending starting points. It is merely

EVERYTHING that is and isn't. And while it seems evident that the next step is to connect that point to another location, there can't be another point. You can't have an alternate version of the ninth-dimensional point, because any description of what the other point is would be a part of the first point. So it would seem that the ninth dimension is the end of the road. And yet...

## 10D

In theory, the tenth dimension kind of exists and it also doesn't. The tenth dimension would be the connecting of two ninth-dimensional points, but every time we try to define the second point, it becomes a part of the first point. But the space in which these points attempt to exist is the tenth dimension. Nothing exists in the tenth dimension that is ten-dimensional, but the full ninth dimension is sitting in the middle of it, all alone.

To recap all of this, we can't (at a single moment) see anything above the third dimension, so while it's fun to think about the future and learn from our past, don't forget to live in the moment.

# WORKSHEET TIME!

Map out your future (only the next hour) fifth-dimensionally. What is every possible path that you could be on from the actions you take over the next sixty minutes? Which two paths seem the farthest from each other, and what made them that way in just 3,600 seconds?

```
    @%
  ]}[%
   {>
 $[(<-
  _>}[
>|!+{(<%
```

# CHAPTER XVIII

## THY GREAT MERCY

ILLUSTRATION BY CHRISTY HALL WATSON

Michael Uzquiano asked me to write a chapter about a couple of topics, and I'm happy to tackle them. He asked for my thoughts on entrepreneurship and my songwriting past. Strap yourself in, because if you haven't figured this out by now, I like talking about myself.

## ENTREPRENEURSHIP

*"Your thoughts on entrepreneurship, bootstrapping your own business, lessons learned, etc. It isn't easy building your own thing. It takes a lot of guts and a pleasant kind of madness. A trunkload of perseverance. A lot of struggle, some wins, lots of rejection, etc. It'd be exciting to learn about your journey through that. Why you did it, what you've learned and how you've grown through it."*

Let me start by saying that I feel embarrassed about answering this because the man asking it is a smart, educated guy who founded a successful software company back before I ever dabbled in being self-employed. I'd love to ask HIM this question way more than the other way around. So, now that I got that out of the way, please read the following with extreme skepticism.

I'm not entirely sure how I feel about entrepreneurship. It's a loaded question, and I have a lot of mixed feelings. Sometimes it's exciting and fun. Sometimes it feels like it's the perfect fit for my personality. Then when I look at pay/work ratio, I realize that I'm not doing it correctly, or it's not what it's cracked up to be. A little backstory on what I do: I'm a freelance creative. That's taken the form of a lot of different "brands," but in the end, I'm creating products or providing services based on me making stuff. The problem with that is that everyone wants to do that. Or, at least it feels that way.

When all my peers were off at college, I was pretty much only focused on writing music. I knew it was possible to make money by making music, but I wasn't concerned with it. Making money wasn't a priority. I wanted to make stuff, and it didn't matter if I got paid or not. I wasn't asking myself, "What music do I need to create to get paid?" It was more like, "I'm going to make whatever music I want, and I'll worry about the money part later." That is a terrible business model. The music industry is cursed because it takes a certain level of professionalism to make a quality product, but if you think too professionally, you realize it's not a wise profession.

Imagine you wanted to start a business designing cat furniture, but then you found out that one in two people enjoy building stuff with their hands. Then you find out that there are hundreds of people in your town who spend their own money making cat furniture, then they give them away for free. Should you start a business in this town making cat furniture? Probably not. The only way it would be a good idea is if you can design cat furniture that is SO good that people would gladly pay you for yours instead of taking someone else's for free. That's not a small margin of talent. You can't make something slightly better than everyone else and expect anyone to pay you when something marginally worse costs nothing.

Slightly more than one in two Americans knows how to play an instrument and when a group of them get together a form a band, they realize it's FUN! They likely work day jobs to pay their bills, but one thing they will always look forward to is band practice night.

When it comes time to book their first gig, the last thing they are worried about is making money. They are concerned about performing well. They are focused on promoting the show. They are curious if their friends are going to come. They are worried about a lot of things, and profit margins is not one of them. They know they collectively spent thousands of dollars on their equipment. They realize they have practiced for countless hours. Deep down, they know the bar is charging a 600% markup on beer. They even know that the soundman gets paid a set amount from the door, regardless of the band's cut. They know that they are the essential ingredient for the event, but also the least-valued part of the business equation. And they don't care because it's fun.

Can you imagine what would happen to other industries if professionals treated themselves this way? Maybe you can. I can. Any job that is so fun people will do it for free is at risk for this sickness.

I got into wedding videography as my first entrepreneurial professional endeavor. I don't count the music, as I never had my head in the right state of mind for making money. Wedding videography seemed like a pretty good compromise in that making videos is fun, but making wedding videos is work. People might make music videos or films for free because it's fun, but no one is going to film a stranger's wedding for free*. It was a job I could enjoy, but still enough of a JOB that I wouldn't have to compete with amateurs*.

And, compared to music, it was terrific! When I first started, I was charging way too little by doing a wedding video for $800. But you have to understand; for a guy that made negative net income from music, and slightly more than $100/day at his day job, the concept of earning $800 for 8 hours of work was a damn good income. Except it wasn't 8 hours of work. I didn't know that going in, but it would be WEEKS of work to edit those weddings. I'd spend tons of money on camera equipment, insurance, licensing, web services, subscriptions, postage, travel, advertising, assistants, and a lot of things I'm forgetting... oh, and TAXES. Jesus, the quarterly estimated tax payments were some depressing sticker-shocks. After several years, I finally calibrated the costs and went from an $800 price tag to around $3000. And while that might seem like a lot, it takes over ten weddings to make a minimum wage annual salary. The most weddings I was ever able to fit into a year was 26. So at best, it's been a lower-middle-class income. At worst, it's been poverty.

It's been poverty for the most part. Or at least it would have been without a safety net. I've been fortunate enough to do this "self-employed experiment" while married to a wonderfully supportive woman who makes a consistent income. Had I been single, I wouldn't have made it to the profitable years, because I would have been homeless and starving before inevitably giving up.

Is entrepreneurship right for most people? It probably is. But do most people have the financial flexibility to lose money for an unknown number of years imminently? No. Adults don't work at Footlocker because it's their passion or their dream career. They do it because they are two months behind on their rent.

*As it turns out, that wasn't true.

What I do LOVE about entrepreneurship is that it can be like water, filling in the crevices of your personality. For me, working for myself doesn't mean doing everything myself. It's about doing what I'm good at and what I enjoy doing and delegating the rest. That's something most people don't get to do at a regular nine-to-five.

My situation is different, in that I can work on things I want to work on, without much concern for profit margins (right now). My primary responsibility these days are to negate the need for expensive childcare, so right now I've been enjoying cramming creative projects into the small gaps in my schedule, like writing, podcasting, and weekend event photography/ videography.

Everything I make at this point is extra income to my wife's breadwinning. However, if for some reason I needed to be the primary source of income for my family, I'm not sure I could do it at this stage. Trying to build something big enough to do that would indeed be a journey into the financial unknown. So, for example, if my wife lost her job, it would make more sense for her to find a new one than for me to try and ramp up my business projects. While the "water" fits into my odd-shaped life perfectly right now, I'm not sure it's "enough" to fill all of my family's financial needs.

I guess I have mixed feelings about entrepreneurship because I've never felt like it is lucrative enough for me to brag about it. It has been profitable enough for me and my role in my family, so I guess that's all that should matter. In a nutshell, it makes more money than it costs, but it's a major time-suck.

It also occurred to me recently that I have no hobbies if a hobby is something you don't accept payments for doing. I do a lot of things for fun, but I take money for doing them. My podcast is fun, but we have ads. My book is fun, but it isn't free. My music albums are for sale online. I can't think of anything I do that isn't a side-hustle (be it highly or barely profitable). And while I might very rarely go bowling, see a movie, or support a local band, it's nothing that constitutes a hobby. While almost everything I do for fun has a framework inside of capitalism, I don't have much money to show for it. That is what entrepreneurship is for me.

## MUSIC

*"I'd personally dig hearing about your songwriting past. Thoughts on song concepts, efforts abandoned, cool chord progressions, influences and so forth. Thoughts on the perfect 3-minute pop song. Songs that perfected the impact of a well-timed key-change. Thoughts on mixing, things you felt worked, things that didn't, the saddest key, your musical influences, etc.!"*

My songwriting past has been as follows: Got a guitar, wrote a terrible song, then wrote a song slightly less terrible, and so on. The first song I ever wrote was titled "Drew Barrymore." It was about Drew Barrymore. Here are the lyrics:

> *"Drew Barrymore was in "E.T."*
> *Drew Barrymore is older than me.*
> *Drew Barrymore was in "Bad Girls."*
> *In that movie, she had blond curls.*
> *Drew Barrymore was in "Boys on The Side."*
> *She settled for girls at the time.*
> *She collects men's phone numbers.*
> *She collects women's phone numbers."*

There might have been more lyrics, but I don't remember what they were. I think I was 13 years old when I wrote it. It was four chords: B5, E5, A5, D5. I wasn't kidding; that's a terrible song. Super cringy lyrics from a pubescent boy who had the hots for Drew, but didn't fully grasp the concept of bisexuality. It was also an era where the punchline to an SNL joke was that someone was gay, so to me and my friends, at the time, these were some hilarious lyrics.

I remember how I used to pick chords at the time. I didn't learn any music theory for years after that, so I wrote chord progressions by choosing patterns. The B-E-A-D pattern from Drew was a square. Root notes: Starting on the seventh fret of the E-string, it moves to the seventh fret on the A-string, down to the fifth fret on the E-string, then over to the fifth fret back on the A-string. Almost all my songs did something like that. Usually four chords, and always drawing a shape on the neck.

Years later, when I took music theory classes, I would feel frustrations from the "rules" of keeping chords and melodies in a key. Everything up to that point had been ignorantly chromatic. I got over the limitations eventually. I still like to mess around in chromatic scales, but it's a little less ignorant now. However, I think one thing that has always been consistent is that I try stuff until I think, "That sounds right. It sounds like it should do that." So honestly, I don't figure out what key I'm in when I write anything. I make sure it sounds right. Learning and practicing scales is a great way to learn what "sounds right."

That said, there is no right and wrong. All the rules are human-made. Saying something "sounds right" is saying it sounds like something you associate with being "good" which isn't real. I highly recommend checking out a thirty-minute YouTube video by "Vihart" called "Twelve Tones." It blew my mind. I don't need to talk about it; watch it. It's worth a half hour of your uninterrupted, undivided attention.

After that, if you want to cleanse the palate of your 12-toned brain, listen to Gregorio Allegri's "Miserere mei, Deus." It will cleanse your mind of the chaos, with soothing harmonies of which your Westernized brain can make sense. It is also the song that contains the most magnificently composed harmony I've ever heard—specifically, the harmonies that occur on the words "misericordiam tuam" which follow the opening lyrics "Miserere mei, Deus secundum magnam..." The full line put together translates to "Have mercy on me, O God, according to Thy great mercy." The harmony I adore falls on just the word "misericordiam." The "tuam" is a nice resolving blend of notes, but the magic happens on "misericordiam." It's easy to spot, as it is the last blending of harmony before the melody switches to a unison Gregorian-style chant for the first time. Yeah, to make things complicated, the parts repeat, but the lyrics change. For notation-location-sake, I'm just referencing the first verse. Here, I've included some manuscript...

I'm a big fan of harmony. In the local Milwaukee original rock scene, I like to think I was one of a small number of dudes who could harmonize live vocals. I wasn't especially good at it, but most people weren't. Maybe it was the years of

Si Canto il Mercoledi, e Venerdi Santo
35
Miserere del Sig.r Gregorio Allegri
Mi_fe_re_re me_ _i, De_ _ _ _us, fecundūm
Magnam mi_feri_cor_ _ _ diam tu_ _ _am.
Magnam miferi-cor_ _ _ diam tu_ _ _am.
Magnam mi_ _feri_ _ _ di_am mi_fe_ri_cordiam tu_ _am.
Magnam mi_ _fe_ri_cor_ _diam mi_feri_cor_ _diam tu_ _ _am.
Magnam mi_ _fe_ri_cor_ _ _ diam tu_ _ _am.

the church choir at Our Lady of Lourdes under the amazing guidance of "Anno Piano" Van Deusen. You know what? This woman deserves her own chapter.

## ANYWAYS, IN CONCLUSION:

I'm a sucker for major or minor third harmonies (the root note and the third note in a scale). Example: B or Bb above a G. A sixth is just an inverted third (G above a B or Bb), so those are almost just as good.

I like when a major chord is followed immediately by the minor version of the same chord. It's a nice key change, but it can be overused, so it's good in small doses.

I'm a sucker for suspended fourth chords or harmonies that resolve into the third. So in G major, a suspended C will create a small amount of tension, which can sound relieving to hear it resolve to a B.

One time I was stuck on a chord that I wanted to have act like a sus4, but the problem was instead of a regular suspended fourth, I had a suspended sharp fourth (which is a little weird). A sharp fourth is a chord going out of key within its scale, so it's dissonant. I learned an alternative to spelling out a dissonant chord such as Fsus#4 (F B C) which resolves to an F major (F A C), was instead doing a C major 11 (F B C E G), and having it resolve to an F major 7 (F A C E). The tension/harmony I was looking for was the BC to AC with a root of F, without adding notes outside the chords' scales. You also get an extra E in there with both chords (and a G in the Cmaj11) that makes them a little more colorful, without compromising the intentions of the resolving melody or root note progression.

A little context: Here are eight chords; each chord gets two beats in 4/4 time...

Asus4, Am, Gsus4, G, Cmaj11, Fmaj7, Esus4, E

With the melody being very predictable...

D, C, C, B, B, A, A, G#

I wrote this when I was 16 years old, using only a piano (I don't play the piano) and blank manuscript paper and a pencil. And help from some of the adult musical mentors in my life (more on that in the next chapter). One thing I've learned over the years when it comes to writing out music is to try and keep things as simple as possible, and not to micromanage the musician reading it. For example: When I described the C major 11, I went on to say it had a root note of F. So, technically, that chord would be a Cmaj11/F. However, I never wrote anything for a single musician to play by themselves. If that chord was being played on a guitar, then the accompanying bass guitar would be playing the F. With those two instrument frequencies being so dynamically different, it doesn't matter what order the notes are in on the guitar, as long as the note-inventory is accurate. So why make the chord harder for the guitarist to interpret, if that root note doesn't even matter? An even more straightforward way of looking at it is if the bass has the F covered, then the Cmaj11 on the guitar doesn't even need an F, as it would be totally tonally redundant. When you take the F out of a Cmaj11, it becomes a Cmaj7 (which is an easier chord to play).

When Ken Uzquiano and I recorded this song (performed by my friends Anne and Sarah) in 1998, I had Sarah play the melody on a violin. If I had asked a guitarist and a bassist to play on that recording (instead of Anno Piano), I wouldn't have even bothered with a Cmaj11/F or even a Cmaj7, because the violin's melody would have covered the B, and the bass would have covered the F. That leaves only a plain old boring C major for the guitar, which is fine. Minimalism is good.

We didn't have a guitar and bass, though. We had the one and only Anno Piano! So she played something even more tonally rich: Instead of a Cmaj11/F resolving to Fmaj7, she played an A minor add2 over F, resolving to A minor over F. That's probably what was the more "correct" way to do it.

In the end, it's about accomplishing your intended purpose. All the little details, theory, arrangements, and what have you, is not as important as making your point.

```
\}%%[
 %_%
 ^>[
 {*%
]{[!(&*{
 &}_
 ~!]
  !
&>>$
]*>~
```

# CHAPTER XIX

SHEPPARD ME, OH ANNO

*I took this photo of Anne in 1998 with my first SLR 35mm camera, the Pentax K1000*

PHOTOGRAPH BY JOHN MARSZALKOWSKI

If anyone deserves to have their praise sung, it's Anne Van Deusen. She is a straight-up gift to the world. I don't know who gave her to us, but we don't deserve her. I remember switching to Our Lady of Lourdes (OLOL) from St. John the Evangelist when I was a preteen. My parents raised me at St. John's, but they didn't care what church I went to as long as I went to a Catholic church. So, once I was old enough, I would walk to OLOL, go to mass by myself, walk home, give mom that week's issue of their church bulletin to prove that I went, and that was that. However, I was in a weird place spiritually, in my teens.

I just came from St. John's where I didn't enjoy going to church. OLOL was terrific by comparison. It's hard to explain, but I'll try: St John's was probably a bunch of old grumpy conservative Catholics, and OLOL was a diverse group of Catholics who enjoyed cultural music, dance, the LGBT community, and all sorts of hippy-shit by Catholic standards of the time. It's like OLOL enjoyed smiling when they went to church, and St. John's didn't. I'm trying to be comedic when I put it like that, but it also makes complete sense in my head. I have only two positive memories of St. John's and that's Brother David playing Johann Sebastian Bach after mass (I special-requested it) and Father Paul's improvisational storytelling.

Okay, anyways, so I was going to OLOL, and it was great by comparison, but I still didn't feel like I belonged. Besides not knowing anyone, I was also in the very beginning stages of losing my religion. The very early stages are the worst because you still believe enough religious stuff to feel incredibly guilty about questioning it. The initial flood of guilt is, assumingly, what keeps the faithful folks faithful. I, on the other hand, felt content drowning in sadness because I deserved it.

At the risk of sounding like a cliché teen: I occasionally thought about suicide. I didn't want to kill myself, but I didn't want to be alive, either. I felt like I was a complete failure, and like a lot of dramatic, emotional kids, I felt like "giving up" was a rational option.

Many Saturday nights I walked to OLOL, didn't go into the church, but grabbed a bulletin, sat in the doorway to a classroom in a hallway where no one would see me, and cried for an hour. I'd think about hell and what it was going to be like when I got there. I'd think about how I was a sinful person, and how the only way to fix it was to be someone I wasn't. I'd cry imagining what my family would think if they knew what I was thinking. But these early stages were hard because there wasn't any confidence in these new ideas. And so, I'd cry in doorways, until that one Saturday when Anne found me.

She had a great approach. While I have no memory of what she initially said, I remember her face and I could tell that she was legitimately concerned for me. She asked me to walk with her. We talked, but I don't remember what about. She showed me her choir room where the youth choir rehearsed. She invited me to join them. I said I wasn't sure if it was a good idea. I didn't know if I believed all the lyrics, and besides that, I didn't know how to sing. I noticed her sister's guitar in the corner. Its case was marked appropriately with her name "Jane Wester" written in what looked like white-out. I commented on it, and she asked if I played. I said something along the lines of "I can't read sheet music, but I know some chords." She excitedly showed me some of their church music, and right above the lyrics and melody was the chords written clear as day, like "C" or "Em." She invited me to try playing along at the next rehearsal.

And I did.

Over the next several years, I would become close friends with my fellow choir members. I would find wisdom in the adult musicians, like Marc, Peg, and Michele. Marc even hired me at his music store selling cassettes and CDs.

Anne taught me to sing. More than that, she taught me how to be confident in singing. I learned how to sing harmony there. She pushed me to play guitar parts that were harder than I thought I could do. She was strict when she knew I could do better, and she was overjoyed when I impressed her.

176

She was an adult, and I was a kid, but she still socialized with me. I saw "Star Wars: The Phantom Menace" in theaters with her and Marc. I had a house party in high school, and they came over and hung out with a bunch of teenagers. My rock band played a charity show at my high school auditorium in 1997, and when the curtain opened, Anne's face was the first I saw.

I still went through some pretty terrible depression in my teenage years, and I still ended up losing my religion, but Anne brought me into a community of some of the most positive people I've ever known. And as corny as it might sound, I have to say in all honesty that Anne saved my life that night in that classroom doorway. I'm not saying she "took the blade out of my hand" or anything that dramatic, but she welcomed me down a path that taught me the value of community. Anne introduced me to a lot of people who would become important to me, and I to them. She made me a better musician, nurtured my fragile self-esteem, and pushed me to be better... to be proud of myself. And Anne strengthened my "spirituality," for lack of a better word. Not the dogmas of religion, but she brought me closer to the community.

"Found My Light" was a song I wrote for a youth concert we did. The words were religious on the surface, but to me, they meant more about my experience in joining that community than just typical Christian lyrics. The light I found wasn't God. The light was a love for "God's creations" and learning to love myself so much that I didn't want to "give up" anymore.

And Anne was the one who helped me find it.

```
        (
      =(]]
   )(})({]}
      @}{
      =_
   <%#-
   *}[{]
```

# CHAPTER XX

## THE WORST-PAYING BEST JOB I EVER HAD

ILLUSTRATION BY THE ELIZABETH GRAMZ

I'm not entirely sure if I can say the company name here without getting sued by someone. I'm not sure who would do the suing since the company no longer exists.

What I will say is that it was the most significant corporate chains of health clubs in America at one point.

Okay, like the chapter title said, this was one of the worst-paying jobs I've ever had. I didn't necessarily deserve more money for what I did, but I couldn't live on the wages, so I was eventually forced to look for a new job that paid more. But I'm jumping too far ahead. Let me go back to the beginning.

I was 19 years old, I believe. I had recently ended month-long employment with a grocery store where I couldn't hack it. I was enjoying not working far more than I ever liked working, so I didn't have too much ambition to find a new job, besides my father saying, *"You can't just NOT work... you have to do something!"* So, the idea of finding a job was kind of in the back of my mind, I guess.

My buddy wanted us to get gym memberships because we were getting tubby and the girls cruising up and down Highway 100 weren't into soft jawlines and thin arms hanging out the car windows. I told him, "I don't have any money or a job, so I can't get a gym membership. But I'll go with you if you want to check out the gym."

It looked very '80s. An old building with no windows, lots of mirrors, people wearing spandex, a faint smell of body odor and a stronger smell of bleach. The manager greeted us. She showed us around the gym, had us sit on some machines and try them, and before long we were sitting in her office with a binder in front of us full of laminated price plan membership options. My buddy was pretty sold on getting buff, but I quickly interrupted the manager with the sad reality that I had no money and no job. She did the only thing she could to get us both to the gym every day. She sold my buddy a membership, and she gave me a job as a janitor.

## PORTER

I came back the next day to interview (for real) for the job. I remember her asking me, "How clean is your room at home?" to which I simply and unprofessionally responded, "Ummmm... Why?"

She said, "Well, I want to know how clean you are. If you can't clean your room at home, why should I believe you will clean the gym well?"

To which I can't believe I said, "Ummmm... No one pays me to clean my room at home, so it's pretty trashed. If someone started paying me to do that, it would be pretty clean, I guess."

She just stared at me. She knew her situation. The company had employed several special-needs workers to clean the gym, and it just wasn't getting cleaned enough... and they weren't about to fire the special needs people for not being able to clean at a not-special level. Plus, she was a sweetheart. She didn't want to fire anyone, and I like to think she liked me and had already decided to hire me before I bombed the interview.

She called the operations manager into the office. He was a two-ton land-monster with arms as big as my legs. He could lift a car's back tires off the ground but struggled not to sweat profusely when movingly even slightly. He wore a stern face into the office, but I would later learn he was just a big teddy bear. I'm pretty sure he just stopped in to make sure I was slightly less handicapped than the current janitorial staff and was quickly satisfied with my cognitive and motor skills.

Here is a story he shared with me when I asked him what his favorite gym story was:

*"I was getting complaints that some guy was washing his underwear in the sink. Over and over again, people would complain, but always to the front desk and, of course, the front desk couldn't tell me who this person was; only that it was happening. One day, I overheard a person complaining. I sent one of the sales*

*guys down. He was pretty aggressive. He brought the guy up to my office. The*
*member was agitated and embarrassed that he confronted him. I asked him,*
*"Were you washing your underwear in the sink?" "Yes," he said, "I do it all the*
*time." I asked, "why do you feel it's ok to do this?" His response was, "No signs*
*are saying I can't." My immediate response was, "No signs are stating not to*
*crap in the sink. Do you think that would be ok?" He said, "well, no" but that*
*guy didn't have to embarrass me." I said, "you should be embarrassed to wash*
*your underwear in the sink. I'll make it clear for you: You can not wash your*
*underwear in the sink, and if you ever do it again, you can no longer come*
*here." That interaction turned into a "corporate complaint." I was asked to*
*apologize to the guy! I didn't. The End."*

The starting pay was $7 per hour, which was terrific, considering minimum
wage at the time was $5.15 an hour. That was about 25% more than they
needed to offer, so I was happy.

At the time of me writing this book, the federal minimum wage is $7.25, so
that would be kind of like being offered around $10 for a job that required no
experience, no degree, and not even passing the job interview.

Anyways, I worked as a "porter," which was a cute name for a janitor. When
you imagine a stereotypical janitor, you probably think of someone pushing
a mop down an already clean hallway, and emptying waste baskets into a
big bin. My job was that, but also cleaning ball sweat off of gym equipment,
cleaning explosive supplement-diarrhea off the walls and backs of toilets, and
all sorts of things I don't want to relive.

My memory of the job was that there was always something to do, there was
no way to get to everything in one shift, so you might as well hang out and
shoot the shit with the receptionist for most of the night.

## RETAIL

Two things happened to my career while I did this job over time:

1. I was almost fired for being a lousy janitor. The gym was filthy, and it was pretty much my fault.
2. I figured out that I preferred talking to members about nutritional supplements and their workouts a lot more than I liked cleaning up diarrhea.

There was even one specific month where I, the janitor, made more nutritional sales than any of the personal trainers. That got me on someone's radar to transfer me to the Downtown location where they had a staffed pro-shop (not just a shelf of products next to the reception desk).

I was no longer cleaning up bodily fluids. I was now in retail. And it wasn't long before I was the manager of that pro-shop. In only a few short years, I had gone from an inexperienced janitor to a manager. The reason was pretty simple: I wasn't good at doing stuff. I was good at talking to people and being helpful. I wasn't the best at sales, but my customer service was pretty good, which resulted in half-decent sales.

## SALES

It was after that time as a retail manager that I became a membership salesman. That was where the big bucks were. Not for me, but for all the other salesmen who were good at sales.

Let me break away from the story for a moment to share with you what I learned about sales at this time in my life. I need to use an analogy because as you've learned by now, parallels are how I take other people's concepts and repackage them as my own. Okay, here is my "two kinds of salesman" analogy:

A man walks into a bakery and says, "I'm looking for some bread." The baker says, "You've come to the right place! Do you know what kind you need?"

The customer responds, "I'm making food for a dinner party tonight, and I think I need some bread as a side."

The baker responds with friendly questions about the meal and the type of event and learns that the man is making a casual pasta dinner. The baker says, "I have some fresh Italian bread about to come out of the oven. I baked parmesan cheese and garlic into the crust, and I think it would be perfect alongside your dinner. I also have these sourdough rolls that would work well served alongside salads."

The customer responds, "Oh, I'm not serving salads tonight. Just the garlic bread will be fine." The customer buys the garlic bread, but not the sourdough. He comes back next week and buys the sourdough, because this time he has made salads, so he already knows what he wants. The end. That's the first salesman example. Or often phrased as, "the product sells itself." It more or less does, but the salesman guides the process by being helpful and informed.

The second sales example goes as follows:

A man walks into an automotive shop and says, "I'm looking for some bread." The mechanic responds, "You've come to the right place! It looks like your front tires are getting a little bald."

You can imagine where it goes from there.

The point is that when the product sells itself, an excellent customer service staff = a superior sales staff. When the product doesn't sell itself, you need aggressive, pushy sales. Gym membership sales were a blend of the two.

On the one hand, the clients contacted us or visited us, because they wanted what we were selling. So, the product started to sell itself. Where it got weird was that what we sold was a relatively bad deal. Memberships that would cost $50-$70/month in 2001 gave you the same thing that current gym memberships offer you for $10-$20/month. On top of that, back then we had two-year contracts for one specific reason: Everyone signs up, and almost no one sticks with it.

Customer service at this job wasn't just guiding potential clients to the services and products that were right for them; it was also dealing with all the people we were "ripping off" for up to two years after we "ripped them off."

Did we rip them off? I don't think I ever did. I've always tried to be a pretty transparent guy. I spent more time going over the contracts with the customers than I was required. Because of this, I didn't have a whole lot of sympathy for people who read their contracts, signed them, and then didn't want to honor them. Continually dealing with people trying to get out of their contracts was not the kind of customer service I enjoyed.

I remember answering the phone one time and getting an irate woman on the phone who was demanding her contract be made void. She was unreasonable, and since I was covering for the receptionist on break, I decided to transfer her to the other available salesman. However; she managed to say one last thing to me before I was able to put her on hold. I do not remember what it was, but I remember I did not like it.

Coincidently, I also liked to make the other salesman's life hard sometimes, in good fun. So after putting the grumpy-cancellation-lady on hold for a few seconds, I picked it back up to add,

"Thank you for holding. Please know that you entered into a signed agreement and there is nothing you can do to get out of it. Please continue to hold."

I then paged the other salesman over the intercom, "Attention Staff, ****; you have a phone call on line two. ****, line two."

Twenty minutes later, he comes up to the front desk from his office and says, "Wow, that woman was distraught!"

I'm not going to lie; we liked to give some members a hard time. Not most of them, though. Most members were our friends. Honestly. They came in on a regular workout schedule, they were friendly, and we were helpful... you know, they were friend-like. I never got a beer with any of them after hours, but I saw them and talked to them more than my regular friends and family. I feel like that status deserves a title. But anyway, like I was saying, most were cool. Some were assholes.

The assholes were the types of members that ran around a dead body on the running track and then got mad because we said they have to stop because the cops and paramedics needed to secure the area. Most members were not like that, but some were.

## FRONT DESK MANAGER

After my time as a salesman, I became... something else. I believe my title at the time was Customer Service Advocate... or something like that. The position was previously referred to as "Front Desk Manager" as this role involved managing a staff of receptionists. There wasn't much to manage. It was pretty much just covering shifts when people didn't show up for work. But it did include one important responsibility, which was auditing the sales contracts and transactions from the previous day and mailing them with all the money to corporate.

As my time as a fancy manager-like receptionist, I would encounter every member face-to-face at one point or another. Like I said, most were great. Some were dicks. I remember there was a personal trainer who I often worked with. We would hang out at the front desk and invent games. One of them was a game where we would try to give the member's membership card back to them in the exact way they gave it to us (to get checked in). Most of the time it went unnoticed by the member, as most members knew how to hand over a card like a civilized person. However, there were a few situations that stand out in my memory.

One thing that happened pretty commonly was that the member would get the card out, you'd reach for it, but they'd drop in on the desk. We would swipe it, they would reach for it, and we'd drop it back on the desk. You get the idea of this game. It involved being a dick, but only an exact mirror of the dick standing before us. One time a card was thrown onto the desk with a little more spunk than a casual flop, and the personal trainer swiped it and then threw the card across the lobby. Everyone, including the member, had to laugh at that one.

Another harmless card interaction would be the member not dropping the card, but instead snapping it on the desk. The cards were thick as a credit card so that it would make an audible snapping sound. So, as you can expect, we'd swipe it, and snap it back. I think it was that same member that got his card chucked across the lobby and the same personal trainer that took this one to the next level as well. Dickhead member snaps the card down as hard as he can. And it was loud this time. Almost a "crack," rather than just a "snap." Of course, the personal trainer swiped his card and preceded to bend his card in half, on purpose. Man, I loved working with that guy.

I think the riskiest move I ever did with the card-mirror game was that some members would reach past your hand and swipe the card themselves. This was a pet peeve of mine, probably because they were reaching into my space. So, one time a client attempted to do this, but for some reason, the card wasn't beeping. I took the card out of their hand, swiped it, reached past their open hand that was waiting to accept the card, and I slid the card back into their wallet that they had placed on the desk counter.

We had all sorts of front desk games. We'd see who could sit the longest on an exercise ball without their hands or feet touching the ground. We'd make up bogus announcements to say over the sound system. We'd make prank calls to other gyms. Heck, one time that trainer and I had a contest on a Sunday (Sundays were always dead slow) where we both ate these Burger King cheeseburgers with four patties of beef, and then we raced to see who could go the longest without shitting in the childcare bathroom.

The childcare toilet was the preferred shitter in the gym because it was close to the front desk, it was continuously cleaned (or at least significantly more than the locker rooms), but also because it saw a lot less traffic than the ones in the locker rooms. That toilet was also extremely low to the ground, which kind of made using it a game in itself.

## OPPORTUNITIES

The absolute zenith of my career at the gym came after I transferred to their Brookfield, WI location (I had been moved around from club to club over the years and had worked at all five of their Milwaukee market locations). Not for what was going on in Brookfield, but for the opportunities that fell into my lap while I was there.

Now, what had happened was, we had a high-up dude working for us at one point, and he left. Then, he came back a couple of years later and was our Regional Vice President all of a sudden. What was that position, you ask? I don't know, exactly. He was everyone's boss in our market, but as for his position on the corporate ladder, it's not like he was second in command to the CEO or anything like that. Remember that scene in the movie American Psycho where all those dudes whip out their business cards to compare them, and they all look almost the same? Did you notice that all of their cards said the same position of "Vice President?" I'm sure it's a similar thing to that.

So, our Regional Vice President (I'm going to call him RVP for short) comes back into the Milwaukee market and doesn't recognize many of the old gang. All his right-hand men are either no longer with the company or have transferred to different markets. But RVP remembers me as that weird protein-selling janitor. So suddenly I become semi-important.

## HUMAN RESOURCES

A few other events happened while I was at Brookfield that lead up to this. First, I should mention that the corporate office for our region was in the same building as the Brookfield gym. It was technically not in the gym, but there was a secret passageway. Second, the company was collapsing from the top down. The company was filing for bankruptcy over and over again but remained open for business. Everyone that was a high-up corporate person either "found a new job all of a sudden" or was let go. The corporate office was empty, except for RVP who was moving into that ghost town.

Part of the downsizing included getting rid of the entire human resources department. The only problem with that was that HR did all of the hiring and firing legal paperwork. RVP had an HR person from the Chicago market drive up and teach ME how to do the new-hire paperwork.

All of a sudden, I'm the only employee in the Wisconsin market that knows the procedure for how to hire employees legally. I found myself doing my actual job less and less, and instead, walking new hires through filling out paperwork before having them watch sexual harassment videos. Not to mention going out to lunch or on business trips with RVP all the time.

## ASSISTANT TO THE REGIONAL VICE PRESIDENT

While it was never an official title, it was indeed a good description of what I was doing, which no one else was.

One day RVP calls me up to the office and says,

"Johnny, can you pack a bag for a couple of days? We have a big management problem that's going to end in a massacre, so I might need to drop you off at a hotel in Illinois for a little while. I'll fill you in on the details on the way."

That sounded fun, so I packed.

We're on our way to Rockford, IL to a gym that was added to the Wisconsin market (for some reason) and RVP filled me in on the game plan:

"Here is what's going to happen. We're going to walk in there like everything is fine. However, it's going to get ugly real fast. I'm going to need you to run this club. The whole damn club. We're canning the general manager, the personal training manager, the front desk manager... I need you to run the whole fucking thing. Can you do that?"

"Yes. Yes, I can."

To make an already long story less-long, let's sum it up like this:

RVP went back to Milwaukee and left me in Rockford. I ended up living in a hotel for two months while I ran the club, interviewed people, hired people, and trained people.

So there you have it. Hired as a Janitor. Transferred to Retail. Promoted to Retail Manager. Transferred to Sales. Promoted to Front Desk Manager. Took on Human Resources responsibilities. And, for a brief two months, I was managing and training an entire club and all of its departments. And do you know how much money I was making by the end? $10/hour. Hired at $7, after years of work and several promotions, I was making absolute shit pay.

I walked into RVP's office and said, "Hey boss, I'm trying to save up to buy an engagement ring for my girlfriend, and I can't do it at $10/hour. I think I'm worth more."

"You are, Johnny. There isn't any room in the budget. I still need to fire more people. I can't pay anyone more."

And so I quit. I got a job working at a vending machine company, and it was the worst job I ever had. Sure, I made a lot more money, but I didn't enjoy it at all. And saying I filled vending machines didn't look nearly as good on my resume as all the gym experience did.

There is so much I'm grateful for when I think back to my gym days, but the paycheck will never be one of them. I guess if there is a moral to this story, it's that the paycheck isn't always the reason to take or leave a job.

```
        (
     + ( - %
     > < %
  * ! < ] > <
  ] > < &
  / % < < _
     ! < $
     = %
```

# CHAPTER XXI

COULD THE EARTH ACTUALLY BE FLAT?

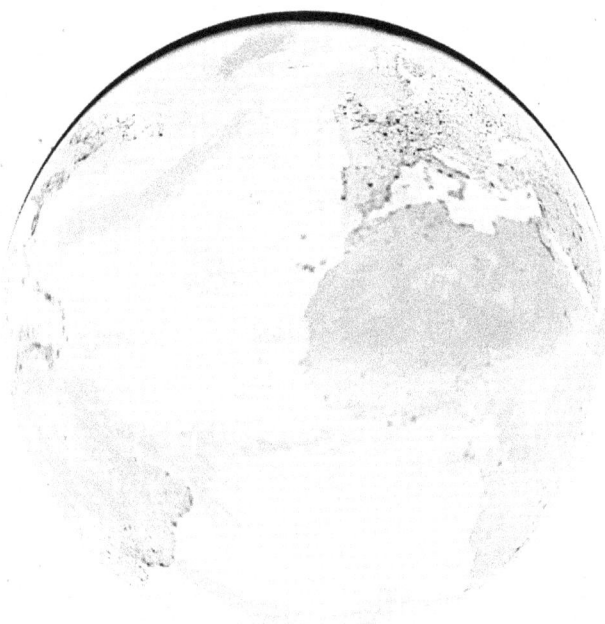

GRAPHIC BY JOHN MARSZALKOWSKI

No.

# WORKSHEET TIME!

If you think the earth is flat, which of the following steps are you willing to take?

- Seek psychological counseling.
- Take an elementary school science class.

# CHAPTER XXII

## THE REASON FOR ALL THIS NONSENSE

ILLUSTRATION BY SARAH HETRICK

$M$y dearest Charlotte:

I hope that when you are old enough to read this book, you'll reach this chapter and look up and across the room, and I'll be there, smiling back.

The idea of possibly not being there for you (due to an untimely death or something) terrifies me now. Not because I don't think you can hack it without me, but because maybe I wouldn't have had time to teach you some basic ideas about how I think the world should work. I am sad, now, thinking about you growing up and not knowing/remembering me. That's why I wrote this really, really dumb book. It's a just-in-case time capsule of pretty much every "important" thing going through my head right now. Just in case.

For every age you grow to be when I am with you, and when I am not, I want you to know the advice your 36-year-old-Dad would have had to give you regarding all the topics of this book.

Education, Depression, Health, Finance, Careers, Politics, Religion, Goals, Parenting, and Love. These are all topics which, if I can't teach you about them, I want you to at least know what I thought about them.

My thoughts do not need to be your thoughts. You get to have your views and opinions in your life. But I want you to know mine and learn from my perspective on the world in which we currently live. Let this terrible book be a reference to you for, "what would Dad say?"

If for some unfortunate reason I'm not there with you as you read this, I hope this book either shows you (or reminds you of) my personality. A goofy, sometimes tacky dude that gets hyper-focused on topics. I'm a know-it-all, but I know very little. I love to talk. I like to try and sound smart, but I want to teach people things they will appreciate. I do all this with a weird sense of humor that never gets me invited to classy dinner parties.

Your mother is so amazing, isn't she? Is she not the best mother you've ever had? Obviously. I can't stop telling people how proud I am of her. Right now (at the time the book is being sold for the first time), you just turned three years old. Your mother is in college, working full time and climbing the business ladder, going to jiu-jitsu consistently, teaching women's self-defense classes, and spending every available second with you. She plays games with you. She gives you constant attention. She gives you baths even when you don't need them, so you can play in the tub (you love baths). She doesn't get enough sleep because you have a hard time going to bed, and you wake up really early. But you make her so happy every moment you are with her. Besides being a super mom, she's such a better wife than I deserve. I won the lottery when she said "yes."

I hope I'm with you when you read this. The chances are good that I will be. Our life insurance provider bet us a quarter of a million bucks that I'll be alive when you're 22 years old, so there is a good chance that none of these ramblings matter. But, just in case. You never know. Life is fragile. Other people and luck can affect anyone. I could play all my cards right and still, for some unfortunate reason, be unable to dance with you at your wedding. That would be a real bummer, but not the end of the world. You could dance with this book... That would be funny.

I have to wrap this up because the book is starting to get to the point where short attention spans will give up if it gets much longer. I need to end on the most important lesson I can think of:

## LOVE

Love is the essential thing in this life. And I don't mean that in some super-romantic, corny way. I mean it like it's the glue to a good life. Respect, loyalty, kindness, empathy—the very fiber of good morality—is a foundation of love. I love you. I love your mother. I love all my family and friends. That is what makes everything worth it in life.

When things aren't going well, and life seems like it might be pointless, I remember that this life is filled with people I love and want to be with. When I think about how insignificant I am in the vast universe, I remember that I am important to the people who love me. There is no meaning of life. There is no official game plan. It is what you make of it, and I can assure you that the BEST parts of anyone's lives are the LOVE in it. If it's what you make of it, then make THAT of it. Make love the point of everything.

Life becomes something more important. It's not just about your survival, but the survival of everyone you love. It's not about the pursuit of only your happiness, but the pursuit of happiness for everyone you love. It's about making sure everyone in your life has what they need. And the bigger you make that circle, the more love there is. Love is not finite. You don't have to divide your heart. Your heart grows. Grow your circle one person at a time, until the whole world is in it.

## IN CONCLUSION

Charlotte, I hope you find this book useful. I made it for you, in a kind of selfish way. I didn't come right out and say this was an instruction manual for life, specifically for you. I wanted other people to buy it. I wanted other people to spend money on it, learn from it and then, when you become old enough, you can enjoy it. Hopefully, if the market was kind to us, by the time you're reading this, there will have been plenty of compound interest in your 529 college savings portfolio from the sales of this book.

I called it "BUY MY BOOK: Not Because You Should but Because I'd Like Some Money" because (besides selfishly wanting to make something that people might like) I wanted some extra money for your college savings. I wanted to make sure I was selling something and not just asking for a handout, so I turned this instruction manual into a book, tried to make it just a tiny bit funny, and put it up for sale. If your Harvard education is entirely funded, then the book did much better than expected. If your tech-school associate degree is fully-funded, the book sold well but maybe a little under target. If public schools have been entirely defunded by the time you're in high school, we probably used up all of the money on a private school by now... Sorry, it looks like you have to go into crippling debt like everyone else who goes to college.

Maybe by the time you're 18, we'll have a socialist government, your university will be paid for with rich people's taxes, and this won't be a concern. But, just in case, we're saving as much as we can for you every month. It's imperative to me that you have a better experience in the education system than I did. I am not a book-smart man. By now, you already know that I'm probably not much help with your homework. I don't know what I can do to make your education go as well as possible. I hate to think that you wouldn't have every possible opportunity to succeed, only because I didn't make enough money. But I'll do everything I can think of. I might not think of anything significant. I'm not the best thinker. I think a lot, but not of anything profitable, usually.

I think about you all of the time. Even when you're in the room with me and I'm working on this book. I should probably stop typing and play with you. In fact, that's what I'm going to do. I'm going to end this book now because I need to cherish every moment I have with you. I'm sorry I spent so much time writing this, but the good news is, it's over.

I'm done. I love you. Let's all live happily ever after.

The end.

```
        (
    & ( | %
      } /
      ! {
 / [ % { { _
   = } # *
% | % [ _ { * ( < &
```

# AFTERWORD

BY DESIREE MARSZALKOWSKI

If you purchased this book, that means that you have been successfully conned by one of the greatest con artists of our time. The author (my husband) has spent countless days, weeks, and months desperately trying to convince you via all forms of media that he is nothing more than an unqualified nobody regurgitating empty words onto blank pages. If you have read this far, you will have realized that he has done nothing more than fail miserably. Instead, John has managed to show everyone glimpses into the many life experiences that make up the wonderful human that has chosen to share his life with me, and I with him. He has shared a lot of very personal stories about his triumphs and struggles that make him who he is. He has also managed to demonstrate all the knowledge he vehemently denies having, from photography and music, to finance and parenting, John will be the first to tell you he is no expert but has not sold that point well.

Throughout his work on this book, I joked (mostly) that he should give the table of contents of this book to a therapist as his initial visit interview. I realized after reading each chapter that writing this book was, in fact, his therapy, and he needed to write it just as much as he needed you to read it.

I think what stands out most about this book is his unwavering ability to use the spotlight that he thrusts himself into, to give others a chance to share and shine in that light. Anyone who knows John can attest that he is definitely a people person, he loves networking and getting to know people and finding ways to show the light he sees in them. This book alone is a testament to that. He reached out and showcased art from artists from all over, even donating an entire chapter to Steve's writing so that he could share in this book. Some of the people that are featured in this book, John had never even met until embarking on this journey.

These gestures go way beyond this book, he may not think so, but the countless sacrifices he has made for our family have not gone unnoticed. Pausing career aspirations and social endeavors so that we can raise our daughter at home and allow me to develop and follow my passions is yet another testament to the great selfless man he is. I hope in reading this book, you got to experience the caring, funny, genuine man the way that I am fortunate to every day.

 I do have one personal confession of my own, however; I told John that I read this entire book, cover to cover. I lied. I did not read chapter seventeen. There is no dimension in which I would read chapter seventeen, sorry honey. I love you.

Stay tuned for the critically acclaimed "BUY MY BOOK: NOT BECAUSE YOU SHOULD, BUT BECAUSE I'D LIKE SOME MONEY" Broadway musical already in pre-production.

# ABOUT THE AUTHOR

By Matthew Kopf
Photo by Jennifer Brindley

John Edward Marszalkowski is a man of many talents. One of which is pretending to be stupid. Though his academic achievements are limited, his capacities are not. In actuality, he is a man of great consideration and compassion. By engaging with life in this way, he enhances the lives of those who know him. *Buy My Book: Not Because You Should, But Because I'd Like Some Money* is his first book. John Edward Marszalkowski lives in Milwaukee, Wisconsin with his wife, daughter, and more animals than you can count.

# ONE LAST THING

Please consider reviewing this book on the website of whichever retailer sold it to you.

If you loved it, then obviously please let the world know. If you hated it, then you owe it to your fellow humans to warn them. Either way.

If you're looking for more ramblings like this book, then please check out http://thisisareal.company/

www.ingramcontent.com/pod-product-compliance
Lightning Source LLC
LaVergne TN
LVHW011223080426
835509LV00005B/286